W9-CCO-223

new food fast

thank you

Catie Ziller, my publisher, for her support, faith and trust. Petrina Tinslay for sharing her talent, patience and total commitment to perfection with me. Vanessa "welcome to my world" Holden—I am very glad you did. Your design talents have taken the book further and thank you for your dedication to having things "just so". Matt Handbury and Murdoch Magazines for their continual strong support of food. To Paula Berge, thank you for keeping my sense of humour going, the props coming in and out, the business operating and, basically, life running. Ben Masters and Briget Palmer—my backbone, recipe testers and photography chefs—thanks for the long haul and your endless enthusiasm. Tony Lee and Smeg Appliances for supplying the total wish list and amazing kitchen for the studio. Shelly and Joy at Mud Australia for indulging me with my own colour of their amazing ceramics in perfect shapes and drop-dead wonderful matt glaze. Dee Bates, simply the perfect PR personified. Susin Chow for your encouragement along the long road of being editor. Thank you for making sense of all those words. Jody Vassallo, thank you for always being there.

Starting with perfect produce helps—a big thank you to everyone at Antico's, Demcos, Paddington Fresh Foods and Mohr Foods; Country Road for their clothes and homewares; Malcolm Greenwood, Global Knives and Dinosaur Designs for the wonderful props.

Thank you Michael Bell, Pinnacle Stainless Steel, Paul Thomas, Jimmy O, Chris and Simon Andrews for building me a studio and kitchen yesterday. My partner Billy for your energy, support, love and building skills—thank you. Thank you to my family.

Author and stylist: Donna Hay
Photographer: Petrina Tinslay
Art Director/Designer: Vanessa Holden
Editor: Susin Chow
Creative Director: Marylouise Brammer

NEW FOOD FAST. Text copyright © by Donna Hay. Photography copyright © 1999 by Petrina Tinslay. Design copyright © by Murdoch Books® . All rights reserved. Printed in China. No part of this book may be used or reproduced in any manner whatsoever without written permission except in the case of brief quotations embodied in critical articles and reviews. For information address HarperCollins Publishers Inc., 10 East 53rd Street, New York, NY 10022.

HarperCollins books may be purchased for educational, business, or sales promotional use. For information please write: Special Markets department, HarperCollins Publishers Inc., 10 East 53rd Street, New York, NY 10022.

Originally published in Australia in 1999 by Murdoch Books® , a division of Murdoch Magazines Pty Ltd.

FIRST U.S. EDITION PUBLISHED 2003

Library of Congress Cataloging-in-Publication Data has been applied for.

ISBN 0-06-056631-0

03 04 05 06 07/10 9 8 7 6 5 4 3 2 1

new food fast

donna hay

photography by
petrina tinslay

WILLIAM MORROW
An Imprint of HarperCollins*Publishers*

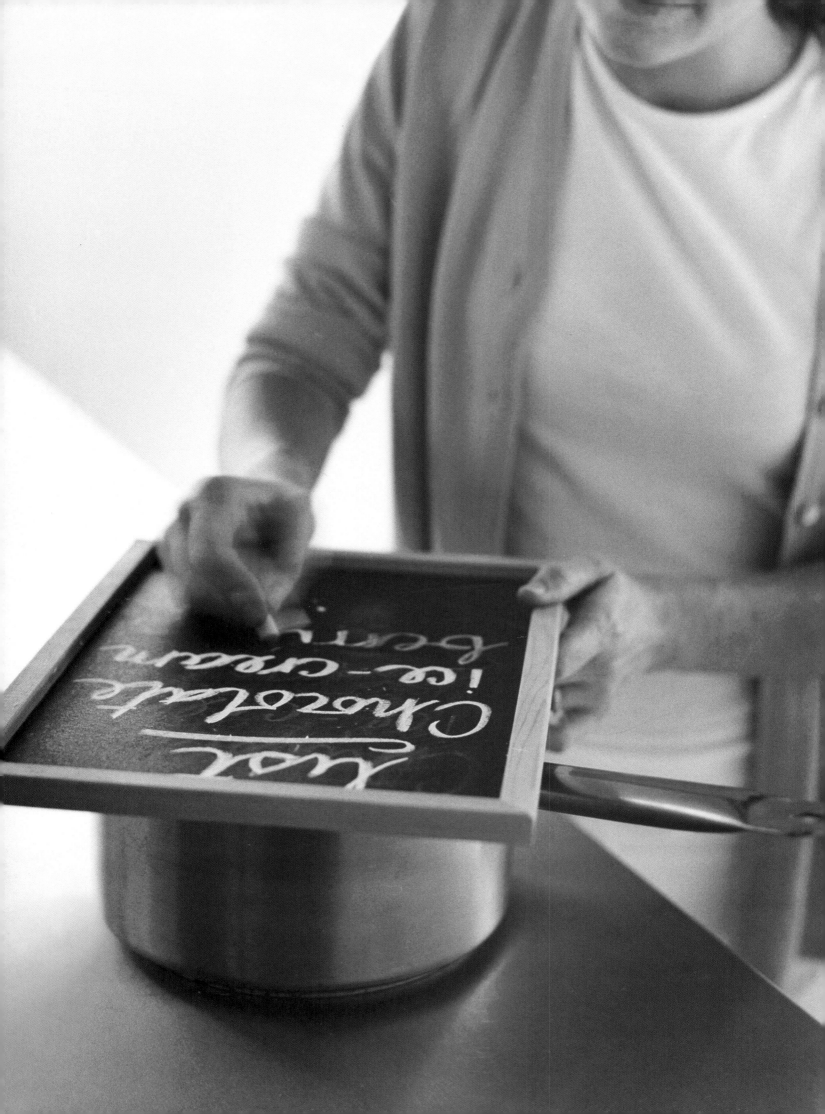

contents

introduction

Time. Today, it makes sense to make clever use of the little bit you have.

new food fast offers stylish and innovative meal-time solutions for busy people—for a fast solo dinner on the sofa or a casual catch-up with friends. From the familiar to the formal, it is full of clever ideas that start at breakfast and take you right through to dinner (and beyond).

Quick-fix classics like pasta are given a modern twist, joined by simple but satisfying flavour combinations, put together with a minimum of fuss. We show you the keys to keeping a well-stocked pantry, catching current produce and utilising straight-forward cooking techniques for no-fuss food in a matter of minutes.

To complement this simple, fresh approach, a comprehensive basics chapter is included, as well as a chapter of quick short top and sides for a range of fresh and delicious menu options. More information about ingredients and cooking terms marked with an asterisk* can be found in the glossary.

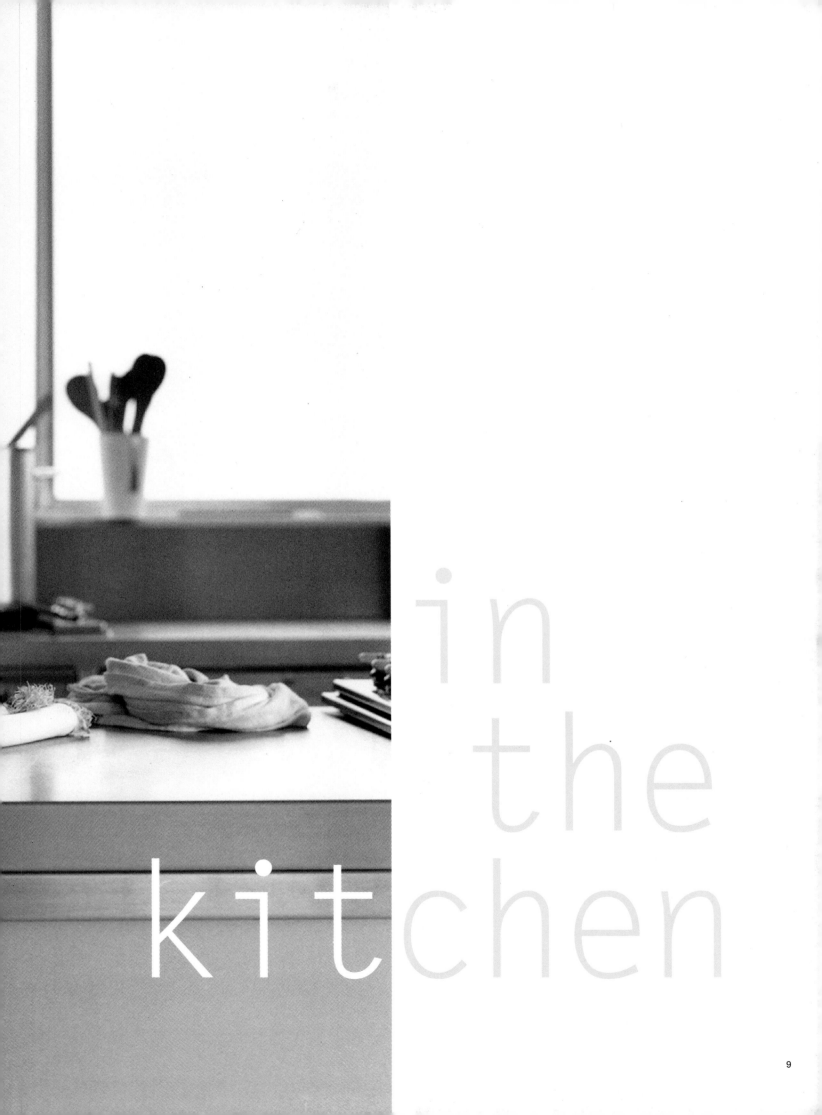

in the

kitchen

shop

Shopping is easier if you have a rough list. Try breaking your shopping into sections to make it quicker and more organised.

staple shop

Make a list so you don't arrive home without things you need. Go through your pantry or try to remember what you have cooked over the previous days so you can restock the staples such as rice, pasta and flour. Shop for meat and chicken up to three days in advance as long as you store it correctly. Purchase fresh vegetables three days in advance. (See store, page 12.)

quick shop

Why not use the Internet to do some of your shopping. Some supermarkets have listings of every product from their shelves for you to choose from a web site. These often include paying by credit card over the Net and delivery —how civil. If you are busy at work all day and you need to do a fast shop on the way home, why not try to place a fax or phone order to your regular butcher, fruit and vegetable providore, fishmonger etc, for a speedy pick-up.

special shop

I like to venture out to the core of ethnic food stores where I can find the best of my speciality shopping. Once every 2–3 months, I stock up on Asian groceries, Italian deli items and pastas, Mediterranean spices, breads and preserves and all those great ingredients the world has to offer.

get fresh

When shopping, buying the freshest and best quality available is important. If you start with good, fresh ingredients then you are more than halfway there. Follow these tips so you can purchase the best quality.

When buying meat, the surface of cut meat such as steaks should be moist and a full deep red colour. The fat should be either a good creamy white colour or a creamy yellow colour which usually comes from grain-fed beef. The fat should also be supple and moist.

Chicken should be plump and firm-looking, not tired and flat. The skin should be moist and will vary from white to yellow for corn-fed chickens. When buying chicken pieces, make sure that they are moist but not sitting in any water or liquid. The flesh should have a pinkish tinge which turns to a green hue when the chicken is spoilt.

Seafood is easy to identify as fresh when you are buying it. All seafood should have a pleasant sea smell. Whole fish should have a clear eye, not clouded. Oysters should be in a cold fridge or packed between ice. The oyster should look plump and moist. Prawns (shrimp) and crustaceans in general should have no discolouration around the legs and a firm intact shell. Do not buy seafood that is sitting in water or in melted ice as the flavour and texture of the seafood will have deteriorated.

Cheese is best purchased from a speciality cheese shop where they should have more knowledge about the cheese, its ripeness and its flavour. Remember when purchasing cheese to have an idea of when you will be serving and eating the cheese. Buy a runny soft ripe Brie for tonight and a Brie with a thin chalky core through it for 4–6 days time.

store

If you have a well-stocked pantry, fridge and freezer then cooking a fast and fresh meal should be a breeze.

pantry

Make sure that your pantry is cool, dark, well-ventilated, and not musty or damp. Organised shelves make it easy to see what ingredients you have. It is a good idea to group ingredients together, such as Asian sauces, rices, pasta, condiments and spices, as you will find the ingredients quickly and it is also easier to prepare a shopping list when foods are grouped.

The pantry is the place where you can store what you need for a quick meal or when friends drop by for a drink and a bite to eat. Cornichons and crackers or oatcakes to serve with cheese and pâté are a great starting point.

snap freeze

Purchased frozen products should be returned to the freezer as soon as possible. If you are freezing foods such as stocks or homemade ice cream, make sure that it is covered well and placed in the coldest part of the freezer with enough clear space around it so the cold air can freeze the food quickly and evenly. The food should be covered tightly to exclude air and to prevent freezer burn which dries the food and makes it very tough. If you wish to chill or freeze food very quickly then use a metal container and cover.

perishables

Meat and chicken will last up to three days in the fridge if removed from the plastic bag and placed on a plate. Cover with aluminium foil or loosely with plastic wrap. Store in the coldest part of the fridge (usually at the back) away from the fridge fan to prevent drying. Fish is best purchased on the day or one day before using because the taste of fresh fish is always best. Place gutted and scaled fish in an airtight container or tightly wrapped in plastic.

I prefer to purchase my vegetables fresh every two or, at the most, three days. Store leafy vegetables wrapped in damp tea towels in the crisper or on the lower shelves of the fridge. Mushrooms should be stored in paper bags so that they can breathe—even the ones you can purchase in plastic trays should be stored in paper or muslin bags. Potatoes should be stored in a cool dark place such as in the bottom of a well-ventilated pantry. Herbs in bunches have a longer life if you snip the stems and place them in a jug of water. Cover them with a damp tea towel or a plastic bag and then store them in the fridge.

Cheese and cured meats often come in plastic. If the wrapping is airtight, there is no need to remove the plastic. Cheese is best stored in a cheesecloth or calico (cotton) bag to prevent it from sweating. Cured meats such as prosciutto should be stored in the deli paper you purchased them in or loosely wrapped in plastic wrap.

Dairy items such as milk should be stored on the fridge shelves and not in the door as most would expect. Because the door is often opened, it is said to be the warmest part of the fridge where the temperature constantly fluctuates. My milk seems to be fine in the door of the fridge—where it fits nicely and looks like it belongs—but my fridge also has a good fan which circulates the cold air, as do most modern fridges.

prep

Get organised and get a head start on the task at hand. You'll cut your cooking time and stress levels when time is of the essence.

prepare to cook

Fill your pantry with basic and convenient stores to save on prep time and get you cooking faster. Start with plain (all-purpose) flour and rice. Sugar in variations from the basic white, caster (superfine) and brown, to demerera* and palm*. Rices such as arborio* (risotto), jasmine, long and short grain. A variety of pastas of different thickness and weight to hold different sauces. Couscous, quick-cooking polenta and lentils are also pantry assets. Olive, sesame, vegetable and chilli oils are a must. A few vinegars like white and red wine, balsamic and cider will also be handy. Quality cooking wine has a better flavour through the food so have a bottle of red, dry white and dessert wine on hand.

Convenient stores include quality bottled tomato pasta sauce, curry* and laksa* pastes, canned Italian plum tomatoes, quality canned tuna in oil, canned beans, anchovies in salt or oil, marinated olives, salted capers and liquid stock.

Fill the fridge with a few cheeses including parmesan, cheddar and maybe a blue or some fresh ricotta, and dairy items such as milk, yoghurt, butter and cream. Many condiments and sauces need to be refrigerated after opening. Great flavour bases or boosters to a meal include condiments such as mustards, horseradish, chutneys, Asian chilli paste, miso* paste and wasabi* paste, and sauces such oyster, soy*, hoisin, sweet chilli, and fish.

get busy

When returning from shopping and before storing, trim steaks of any fat or sinew, trim and prepare chicken, and clean, rinse and pat dry seafood. Trim and chop vegetables and greens, cover them well and store in the fridge until required. To revive salad greens before serving, place in bowls of cold water with a few cubes of ice to refresh.

Shred ginger, chop chillies and garlic or slice onions and store in separate little bowls covered tightly with plastic wrap in the fridge. Freeze lemon or lime juice in ice cube containers to save time and effort later.

Foods to be marinated can be prepared ahead of time, as long as you are not marinating meat, chicken or fish in lots of acid, like vinegar or lemon juice, for more than 2–3 hours. The acid will break down the texture of meat.

Remove foods such as cheese, chocolate and rich chocolate cakes from the fridge so that they have plenty of time to return to room temperature and will have regained their full flavour when served.

time wise

There are some things that definitely need to be cooked just before serving time. If serving hot, cook meat, chicken or seafood just before serving—reheating is drying and not ideal.

Chop herbs such as parsley, chervil, mint and basil so that they have a fresh full flavour and are not discoloured. Always dress a leaf salad last, as the dressing often makes the leaves soggy if allowed to stand for any amount of time.

food fast

10 minutes (or so)

panini

couscous

noodles

wraps

egg rolls

pasta

melts

steamed greens

lemongrass broth

sashimi

egg rolls

pasta with fresh tomato and rocket sauce

mussels in ginger and lemongrass broth

egg rolls

2 teaspoons sesame oil
4 green onions (scallions), chopped
4 eggs
fillings such as smoked salmon, smoked chicken, rocket
(arugula), baby English spinach, chopped tomato
thick sweet soy sauce to serve

Heat the sesame oil in a large, non-stick frying pan over medium heat. Add the onions and cook for 2 minutes. Remove half the onions and set aside.
Beat the eggs lightly to combine them. Add half the egg to the pan and swirl to evenly coat the base. Cook for 2–3 minutes or until almost set. Slide the egg from the pan and place fillings of your choice down one side. Roll up and serve with thick soy. Return the remaining onions to the pan and make a second egg roll. Serves 2.

pasta with fresh tomato and rocket sauce

400g (14 oz) fresh pasta*
5 very ripe roma* or ox-heart tomatoes, finely chopped
2 teaspoons salted capers, rinsed
¼ red onion, finely chopped
2 tablespoons olive oil
3 tablespoons shredded basil
2 cups roughly chopped rocket (arugula)
200g (6½ oz) fresh ricotta cheese
cracked black pepper
parmesan cheese to serve

Place the pasta in a saucepan of boiling salted water, cook for 4–5 minutes or until al dente, and drain.
Combine the tomatoes, capers, onion, oil, basil, rocket, ricotta and pepper. Toss through the hot pasta and sprinkle with the parmesan. Serves 4.

mussels in ginger and lemongrass broth

3 cups (24 fl oz) fish stock
2 tablespoons shredded ginger
2 stalks lemongrass*, finely chopped
2 teaspoons shredded lemon rind
1kg (2 lb) mussels, cleaned

Place the stock, ginger, lemongrass and lemon rind in a saucepan over high heat. Bring the broth to the boil then add the mussels and cook for 2–3 minutes or until they have opened. Discard any mussels that do not open. Serve in deep bowls with the broth and some bread. Serves 4.

sashimi on gingered noodle salad

tuna sashimi* for 4 people
soy sauce and wasabi paste* to serve
gingered noodle salad
250g (8 oz) dry cellophane (beanthread) noodles*
⅓ cup pickled ginger
2 cups small watercress sprigs
3 tablespoons roughly chopped coriander (cilantro)
3 tablespoons soy sauce
2 tablespoons sesame seeds

To make the gingered noodle salad, place the cellophane noodles in a bowl of boiling water and soak for 2 minutes. Drain.
Toss the noodles with the ginger, watercress, coriander, soy and sesame seeds.
Place the noodle salad on serving plates and top with slices of tuna sashimi. Serve with soy sauce and wasabi. Serves 4.

lamb cutlets with chilli noodles

8–12 lamb cutlets
oil
cracked black pepper
chilli noodles
1 tablespoon sesame oil
1 tablespoon chilli oil*
3 red chillies, seeded and chopped
2 tablespoons shredded ginger
2 cloves garlic, sliced
3 tablespoons basil or Thai basil* leaves
400g (14 oz) fresh rice noodles*, rinsed under hot water
soy sauce to serve

Brush the cutlets with oil and sprinkle with pepper. Cook under a preheated hot grill (broiler) or in a hot frying pan for 1–2 minutes on each side or until cooked to your liking. While the cutlets are cooking, heat the sesame and chilli oils in a wok or frying pan over high heat. Add the chillies, ginger, garlic and basil and cook for 1 minute. Add the noodles and cook for 3–4 minutes or until heated through. Serve the noodles with the lamb cutlets and small bowls of soy sauce on the side. Serves 4.

sashimi on gingered noodle salad

lamb cutlets with chilli noodles

pasta with smoked salmon and dill sauce

asparagus with tofu and balsamic butter

squid with green chilli and kaffir lime leaves

pasta with smoked salmon and dill sauce

400g (14 oz) fresh fettuccine or linguine*
4 tablespoons olive oil
2 tablespoons lemon juice
1 tablespoon salted capers, rinsed
1 tablespoon wholegrain mustard
1/2 red onion, finely sliced
8–10 slices smoked salmon
2 tablespoons chopped dill
2 tablespoons chopped flat-leaf parsley

Place the pasta in a large saucepan of boiling salted water over high heat and cook for 5 minutes or until al dente. While the pasta is cooking, place the oil, lemon juice, capers, mustard and onion in a small saucepan over low-medium heat and cook for 2 minutes or until heated through. Drain the pasta and place on a large serving plate. Toss through the oil and lemon mixture, salmon, dill and parsley. Serve with lots of cracked black pepper and a salad of baby English spinach. Serves 4.

asparagus with tofu and balsamic butter

1 tablespoon oil
2 cloves garlic, sliced
60g (2 oz) butter
3 tablespoons balsamic vinegar
3 tablespoons water
1 bunch asparagus, trimmed and halved
cracked black pepper
4 thick slices firm silken tofu
1 tablespoon thyme sprigs

Heat the oil in a frying pan over medium heat. Add the garlic and cook for 1 minute. Add the butter, balsamic and water and cook for 1 minute. Add the asparagus and pepper and cook for 4 minutes or until tender. Place the asparagus in bowls. Add the tofu and thyme to the pan and cook for 30 seconds each side or until heated through. Place the tofu on top of the asparagus and serve with the balsamic butter. Serves 2.

squid with green chilli and kaffir lime leaves

12 baby squid, cleaned and halved■
1 green chilli, seeded and chopped
4 kaffir lime leaves*, finely shredded
2 tablespoons olive oil
sea salt and cracked black pepper
salad greens, lime and avocado to serve

Place the squid, chilli, lime leaves, olive oil, salt and pepper in a bowl and mix to combine. Preheat a grill (broiler) or barbecue to high heat. Place the squid on the grill, a few pieces at a time, and cook for 10 seconds each side or until just charred. Serve with salad greens, lime wedges and avocado. Serves 4.
■ Ask your fishmonger to clean the squid for you—it's easier and tidier than doing it at home.

lamb with quince glaze

600g (1 1/4 lb) lamb backstrap or eye of loin
1 tablespoon oil
3 tablespoons quince paste*
2/3 cup (5 1/2 fl oz) dry white wine
cracked black pepper

Trim the lamb of any fat or sinew. Heat the oil in a frying pan over high heat. Add the lamb and cook for 1–2 minutes each side or until well sealed and browned. Remove from the pan and place on a plate. Reduce the heat to medium, add the quince paste, wine and pepper to the pan and simmer for 2 minutes or until the glaze has thickened slightly. Simmer the lamb in the quince glaze for an extra minute each side or until cooked to your liking. Slice the lamb into large pieces and serve with the quince glaze and steamed asparagus or salad greens, and wedges of a nutty, soft blue-vein cheese. Serves 4.
note – this lamb dish is great served with the rocket (arugula) salad with warm walnut dressing and olives on page 134 of the short top + sides chapter.

lamb with quince glaze

white fish with pine nut brown butter

pasta with shredded chicken and fried basil

crisp eggplant salad

white fish with pine nut brown butter

100g (3½ oz) butter
2 tablespoons lemon juice
3 tablespoons pine nuts, roughly chopped
4 firm white fish fillets, such as blue-eye cod or swordfish
steamed greens and lemon wedges to serve

Melt the butter in a large frying pan over medium heat until a light golden colour. Add the lemon juice and pine nuts and cook for 1 minute. Add the fish and cook for 2 minutes each side or to your liking.
Serve on steamed greens with the brown pine nut butter as a sauce and with lemon wedges. Serves 2.
note – you could also serve the fish with the iceberg salad on page 134 of the short top + sides chapter.

pasta with shredded chicken and fried basil

400g (14 oz) fresh pasta*
1 tablespoon olive oil
3 chicken breast fillets, halved
2 tablespoons olive oil, extra
¼ cup basil leaves
125g (4 oz) fetta cheese, chopped
cracked black pepper

Place the pasta in a saucepan of boiling salted water and cook for 4–5 minutes or until al dente.
While the pasta is cooking, heat the oil in a large frying pan over medium-high heat. Cook the chicken for 2–3 minutes each side or until cooked through. Remove, cool slightly and shred the chicken.
Add the extra oil to the pan and heat. Add the basil and cook for 2 minutes or until crisp. To serve, drain the pasta and toss with the chicken, fetta and pepper. Pour over the oil and fried basil and serve with lemon wedges. Serves 4.

crisp eggplant salad

1 eggplant (aubergine), thinly sliced
olive oil
1 baby cos (romaine) lettuce, halved
150g (5 oz) marinated fetta cheese with oil, crumbled
2 tablespoons basil leaves, torn
cracked black pepper

Brush the eggplant well with olive oil. Place in a frying pan over medium-high heat and cook for 2–3 minutes each side or until golden and crisp.
Place the lettuce on plates and top with eggplant slices, fetta, basil and pepper.■ Drizzle with the flavoured oil from the fetta and serve. Serves 2.
■ You could also grill (broil) some thinly sliced prosciutto until crisp and serve as part of this salad.

pasta with scallops and lemon butter

220g (7 oz) fresh pasta*
60g (2 oz) butter
1 tablespoon oil
2 teaspoons shredded lemon zest
cracked black pepper
10 scallops■
1 cup chervil* sprigs

Place the pasta in a saucepan of boiling salted water and cook for 4–5 minutes or until al dente.
While the pasta is cooking, melt the butter and oil in a frying pan over medium heat. Add the lemon zest and pepper and cook for 1 minute or until the zest is soft. Add the scallops and cook for 20–30 seconds each side or until sealed.
To serve, drain the pasta and toss with the chervil. Top with the scallops and the lemon butter sauce. Serves 2.
■ This recipe is also great with prawns or cubes of fish such as salmon instead of the scallops.

pasta with scallops and lemon butter

rocket and parmesan couscous salad

1 cup couscous
2 cups (16 fl oz) chicken or vegetable stock, boiling
2 tablespoons butter
1/4 cup grated parmesan cheese
cracked black pepper
200g (6 1/2 oz) rocket (arugula) leaves, trimmed
4 vine-ripened tomatoes, sliced
3 tablespoons balsamic vinegar

Place the couscous in a bowl and pour over the boiling stock. Top with the butter, cover with plastic wrap, and allow to stand for 4 minutes or until the stock has been absorbed. Stir the couscous with a fork and then stir in the parmesan and lots of cracked black pepper.
Place the couscous on plates, top with the rocket and tomatoes and sprinkle with the balsamic vinegar. Serves 4.

balsamic glazed steaks

2 tablespoons olive oil
3 tablespoons balsamic vinegar
cracked black pepper
2 fillet steaks, 2–3cm (3/4–1 1/4 in) thick
salad greens, sliced red onion and tomato to serve

Combine the olive oil, balsamic vinegar and pepper in a shallow dish. Place the steaks in the marinade and allow to stand for 2 minutes each side.■
While the steaks are marinating, heat a grill (broiler) pan or a barbecue to high heat. Place the salad greens, onion and tomato on plates.
Place the steaks in the hot pan and cook for 1 minute each side or to your liking. Brush with the marinade while cooking. Place the steaks on top of the salad and serve. Serves 2.
■ Do not leave the steaks in the marinade too long as the acid will change the texture of the meat.

chilli steak wraps

500g (1 lb) rump steak
1–2 tablespoons Asian chilli paste
8 flour tortillas*, warmed
3/4 cup prepared hommus*
8 lettuce leaves
2 tomatoes, chopped
1/2 red onion, chopped
chilli sauce

Trim the steak of any fat or sinew. Spread the chilli paste over the steak. Cook the steak on a preheated hot grill (broiler) or barbecue for 1–2 minutes each side or until cooked to your liking.
While the steak is cooking, spread the warmed tortillas■ with the hommus and top with the lettuce, tomato and onion. Slice the steak, place on the salad and top with some chilli sauce. Wrap one end of the bread to enclose the bottom of the filling and then fold over the sides to enclose. Serves 4.
■ Warm the tortillas in the microwave or covered in a warm oven.

miso soup with chicken and noodles

4 tablespoons white miso paste*
2 teaspoons fish sauce*
2 tablespoons soy sauce
6 cups (48 fl oz) hot water
2 chicken breast fillets, sliced
100g (3 1/2 oz) Asian greens
200g (6 1/2 oz) fresh Hokkien noodles*

Place the miso, fish sauce, soy sauce and water in a saucepan over high heat and bring to the boil. Reduce the heat to a simmer, add the chicken slices and cook for 1 minute. Add the greens and noodles and cook for 2 minutes or until the noodles are tender.
To serve, ladle the soup into bowls. Serves 4.

rocket and parmesan couscous salad

chilli steak wraps

balsamic glazed steaks

miso soup with chicken and noodles

crisp prawns with iceberg salad   hoisin pork in green onion pancakes

swordfish fried in sage olive oil

crisp prawns with iceberg salad

12–14 medium-sized green (raw) prawns (shrimp), shells intact
oil for shallow-frying
1 cup rice flour
1 tablespoon ground cumin
2 teaspoons chilli powder
sea salt and cracked black pepper
chopped chilli and extra sea salt to serve
iceberg salad
1 iceberg lettuce heart
3 tablespoons olive oil
2 tablespoons lemon juice
2 teaspoons Dijon mustard
cracked black pepper

Rinse the prawns and drain. Place oil for shallow-frying in a frying pan over high heat. Toss the prawns in the combined rice flour, cumin, chilli powder, salt and pepper and shake away any excess. Place the prawns, a few at a time, in the hot oil and cook for 1 minute each side or until crisp. Drain on paper towel.
To make the iceberg salad, halve the lettuce and place on plates. Combine the oil, lemon juice, mustard and pepper and pour over the lettuce. Sprinkle the prawns with chopped chilli and salt and serve with the salad. Serves 2.

hoisin pork in green onion pancakes

2 teaspoons sesame oil
600g (1¼ lb) pork fillet
frozen, readymade green onion pancakes■
6 green onions (scallions), sliced
hoisin sauce*

Heat the oil in a frying pan over medium heat. Add the pork and cook for 3 minutes each side, or until almost cooked through.
While the pork is cooking, heat the green onion pancakes following the packet directions and keep warm in the oven. To serve, slice the pork. Place a small pile of onions on each pancake. Top with the pork and hoisin sauce and roll up the edges to enclose the filling. Serve with steamed greens. Serves 4.
■ Green onion pancakes can be found in the freezer section of Chinese or Asian supermarkets. You can also purchase them already cooked from most Chinese barbecue shops. If you have the time, use the crepe batter recipe on page 165 of the basics chapter and add ¼ cup chopped green onions (scallions).

swordfish fried in sage olive oil

3 tablespoons fruity olive oil
2 tablespoons sage leaves
2 teaspoons grated lemon rind
cracked black pepper
4 thin swordfish steaks■

Heat the oil in a large frying pan over medium-high heat. Add the sage, lemon rind and pepper and cook for 2 minutes or until the sage is crisp. Add the swordfish to the pan and cook for 1 minute each side or until almost cooked through.
Serve the swordfish with the sage oil. Serves 4.
■ This recipe suits any type of firm white fish.
note – this dish is great served with the salt and rosemary baked potatoes on page 134 of the short top + sides chapter.

white bean and tuna salad

125g (4 oz) baby English spinach leaves
375g (12 oz) can cannellini beans, drained
375g (12 oz) can tuna in oil, drained
1 Lebanese cucumber, chopped
2 tomatoes, chopped
2 tablespoons chopped flat-leaf parsley
2 tablespoons olive oil
2 tablespoons lemon juice
cracked black pepper

Divide the spinach, beans, tuna, cucumber, tomato and parsley between 4 plates.
Combine the oil, lemon juice and pepper and pour over the salad. Serve with bread. Serves 4.

white bean and tuna salad

peppered beef and cucumber salad

warm tuna panini   prawn salad with parmesan dressing

peppered beef and cucumber salad

550g (1 lb 2 oz) rump or topside steak
oil
cracked black pepper
salad
150g (5 oz) baby English spinach leaves
2 Lebanese cucumbers
2 green onions (scallions), chopped
2 tablespoons chopped flat-leaf parsley
2 tablespoons white wine vinegar
1 tablespoon sesame oil

Brush the steak with oil and sprinkle with pepper. Cook on a hot barbecue, under a grill (broiler) or in a hot frying pan for 1–2 minutes each side or to your liking. Place on a plate and cover for 2 minutes to rest the meat.
While the steak is cooking, place the spinach leaves on plates. Slice the cucumbers into strips with a vegetable peeler and combine with the onions, parsley, vinegar and sesame oil.
Slice the meat and place on the spinach. Top with the cucumber salad and serve. Serves 4.

warm tuna panini

2 round Turkish breads
¼ cup whole-egg mayonnaise
1 tablespoon lemon juice
1 tablespoon chopped dill
375g (12 oz) can tuna in oil, drained
50g (1¾ oz) baby English spinach leaves
1 tomato, sliced
sea salt and cracked black pepper
olive oil

Halve the Turkish bread and spread the bottom halves with the combined mayonnaise, lemon juice and dill. Top with the tuna, spinach, tomato, salt and pepper, and then the Turkish bread tops.
Heat a little olive oil in a frying pan over medium heat. Place the sandwiches in the pan and weight each one with a small plate and something heavy (like a can of tomatoes). Cook for 4 minutes each side or until golden. Serves 2.

prawn salad with parmesan dressing

550g (1 lb 2 oz) cooked prawns (shrimp), peeled
1 cos (romaine) lettuce, separated
1 avocado, quartered
1 tomato, chopped
2 tablespoons salted capers, rinsed
parmesan dressing
¼ cup grated parmesan cheese
½ cup whole-egg mayonnaise
2 tablespoons oil
3 tablespoons lime juice
cracked black pepper

Arrange the prawns, lettuce, avocado, tomato and capers on plates. Combine the parmesan, mayonnaise, oil, lime juice and pepper and pour over the salad. Serve with bread and lime wedges. Serves 4.

chilli pasta with lemon tuna

400g (14 oz) fresh chilli linguine* or angel hair pasta*■
300g (10 oz) sashimi tuna*■■
3 tablespoons lemon juice
2 tablespoons oil
1–2 teaspoons wasabi paste*
2 tablespoons chervil* sprigs
cracked black pepper

Place the pasta in a large saucepan of boiling salted water and cook for 4–5 minutes or until al dente.
While the pasta is cooking, chop the tuna into small cubes. Combine the lemon juice, oil and wasabi. Drain the pasta and toss with the tuna, chervil and lemon juice mixture. Top with pepper and serve with a leaf salad. Serves 4.
■ If fresh pasta is not available, use 400g (14 oz) dry pasta, but the recipe will take a little longer than 10 minutes.
■■ You can also use salmon or ocean trout in this recipe.
note – serve with the iceberg salad on page 134 of the short top + sides chapter to make a complete meal.

chilli pasta with lemon tuna

spinach salad with warm garlic dressing

grilled honey mustard and smoked ham flatbreads

pasta with chicken and spinach

spinach salad with warm garlic dressing

250g (8 oz) baby English spinach leaves
1/2 cup semi-dried tomatoes*
12 slices sourdough baguette
olive oil
warm garlic dressing
3 tablespoons olive oil
3 cloves garlic, sliced
2 tablespoons salted capers, rinsed
1/4 cup Ligurian olives
2 tablespoons lemon juice
2 tablespoons thyme leaves
cracked black pepper

Place the spinach leaves and tomatoes on plates. Place the baguette slices on a tray and drizzle with a little oil. Place under a hot grill (broiler) or on a grill pan and toast for 1 minute each side or until golden.
To make the dressing, place the oil in a saucepan over medium heat. Add the garlic and cook for 1 minute or until lightly browned. Add the capers, olives, lemon juice, thyme and pepper and cook for 1 minute or until heated through. Pour the warm dressing over the salad and top with the grilled baguette. Serves 4.

grilled honey mustard and smoked ham flatbreads

2 tablespoons honey
3 tablespoons Dijon mustard
4 flatbreads
6–8 slices double-smoked ham
6–8 slices ripe Brie
4–6 radicchio leaves
olive oil

Combine the honey and mustard and spread over two of the flatbreads. Top with the ham, Brie and radicchio. Top with the remaining flatbreads and brush with a little oil. Place under a hot grill (broiler) or in a grill pan and cook for 1–2 minutes each side or until crisp and golden. Serves 2.

pasta with chicken and spinach

400g (14 oz) fresh pasta*
2 1/2 cups bottled tomato pasta sauce or classic tomato sauce (see page 146 of basics chapter)
3 chicken breast fillets, sliced
150g (5 oz) baby English spinach leaves
cracked black pepper
parmesan cheese to serve

Place the pasta in a saucepan of boiling salted water and cook for 4–5 minutes or until al dente.
While the pasta is cooking, heat the tomato sauce in a frying pan over high heat. When the sauce is bubbling, add the chicken slices. Cover and cook for 2–3 minutes or until the chicken is cooked.
To serve, drain the pasta, place on plates and top with the spinach leaves. Top with the chicken and tomato sauce and serve with pepper and parmesan. Serves 4.

grilled prosciutto sandwiches

4 slices sourdough or Turkish bread
butter
3 bocconcini*, sliced
2 tablespoons basil leaves
8–12 slices prosciutto*
1–2 tablespoons grated parmesan cheese
cracked black pepper
figs and rocket (arugula) leaves to serve

Place the sourdough slices under a preheated medium grill (broiler) and toast one side. Turn the bread and spread with butter. Top with the bocconcini, basil, prosciutto, parmesan and pepper and place under the grill for 1 minute or until the parmesan has melted and the prosciutto is crisp.
Serve the grilled sandwiches with figs and rocket.
Serves 4.
note – make a larger meal of these sandwiches by serving with the roast tomato salad on page 134 of the short top + sides chapter.

grilled prosciutto sandwiches

chocolate fudge sauce for ice cream   white chocolate tiramisu stone fruit and berries in muscato   amaretto french toast

chocolate fudge sauce for ice cream

½ cup (4 fl oz) cream (single or pouring)
125g (4 oz) dark chocolate, chopped
vanilla bean, chocolate or toffee ice cream

Place the cream in a saucepan over medium heat and cook until hot. Remove from the heat and add the chocolate, stirring until smooth. Cool slightly and pour over your choice of ice cream. Makes 250ml (1 cup).
note – store any leftover sauce in the fridge and warm gently when needed.

white chocolate tiramisu

150g (5 oz) thin Italian sponge finger biscuits
¼ cup (2 fl oz) strong espresso, chilled
¼ cup (2 fl oz) coffee liqueur
¾ cup (6 fl oz) thick cream
white chocolate shavings

Pile the sponge finger biscuits on plates. Drizzle with the combined espresso and liqueur. Top with the cream and white chocolate shavings. Serves 4.

stone fruit and berries in muscato

2 plums, quartered
2 peaches, halved
150g (5 oz) blueberries
150g (5 oz) raspberries
1½ cups (12 fl oz) chilled muscato d'asti wine*

Place the fruit in serving bowls. Top with the well-chilled muscato and serve with a knife, fork and large spoon for the juice. Serves 4.

amaretto french toast

1 egg, lightly beaten
2 tablespoons amaretto*
2 tablespoons caster (superfine) sugar
1 teaspoon vanilla extract
½ cup (4 fl oz) milk
butter
3 slices bread, crusts removed and halved
icing (confectioner's) sugar or maple syrup to serve

Place the egg, amaretto, sugar and vanilla in a bowl and whisk to combine. Whisk in the milk.
Heat a frying pan over medium heat and grease with a little butter. Dip a few pieces of bread into the egg mixture and place in the hot frying pan. Cook for 2 minutes each side or until golden. Repeat with the remaining bread.
Serve dusted with icing sugar or drizzled with maple syrup and small glasses of amaretto and coffee. Serves 2.

figs in vanilla port

¼ cup sugar
¾ cup (6 fl oz) quality port
1 teaspoon vanilla extract
4 figs, halved

Place the sugar, port and vanilla in a frying pan over low heat and stir until the sugar is dissolved. Allow to simmer for 1 minute.
Place the figs in bowls and pour the vanilla port over them. Serve with thick cream or toffee ice cream. Serves 4.
note – if you have the time, make the coconut macaroons on page 126 of the short top + sides chapter and serve on the side.

figs in vanilla port

20

minutes

frittata

udon soup

laksa

rice pilaf

salads

mash

stir fry

harissa

bruschetta

lentils

fried chicken with goat's curd

udon soup with grilled chicken

crisp pancetta baked pork fillet

fried chicken with goat's curd

4 chicken breast fillets, skin on
100–150g (3½–5 oz) goat's curd■
sea salt and cracked black pepper
2 tablespoons oil
2 tablespoons lemon thyme sprigs

Make a pocket in each chicken breast between the skin and the flesh. Fill the pocket with goat's curd using a teaspoon or small spatula. Sprinkle the skin of the chicken with salt and pepper.
Heat the oil in a frying pan over medium-high heat. Add the lemon thyme and cook for 1 minute. Place the chicken, skin-side down, in the pan and cook for 3–4 minutes or until well browned. Turn the chicken and cook for 1–2 minutes or until cooked through. To serve, slice the chicken into large pieces and place on plates. Pour over the lemon thyme oil pan juices and serve with a simple salad or steamed greens. Serves 4.
■ If you prefer, use thick mascarpone instead.
note – try serving this with the asparagus with balsamic butter on page 134 of the short top + sides chapter.

udon soup with grilled chicken

3 cups (24 fl oz) chicken stock
2 tablespoons miso paste*
300g (10 oz) fresh udon noodles*
2 chicken breasts, sliced
oil
2 green onions (scallions), sliced
80g (2¾ oz) enoki mushrooms

Place the chicken stock and miso in a saucepan over high heat and bring to the boil. Reduce the heat, allow to simmer and add the noodles.
Brush the chicken slices with oil and cook under a hot grill (broiler) or in a grill pan for 1 minute each side.
Add the onions and mushrooms to the soup. To serve, ladle the soup into bowls and top with the grilled chicken. Serves 2.
note – enoki are mild-flavoured mushrooms. They can be substituted with any other mild varieties, such as oyster mushrooms.

crisp pancetta baked pork fillet

12–14 slices pancetta*■
350–400g (11–14 oz) pork fillet
1 apple, sliced
2 teaspoons oil
2 tablespoons sage leaves
cracked black pepper

Preheat the oven to 220°C (425°F). Wrap the pancetta around the pork fillet to enclose. Place the sliced apple in the base of a baking dish and top with the pork. Sprinkle with the oil, sage and pepper. Bake for 12–15 minutes or until the pork is cooked to your liking. Serve with a peppery rocket (arugula) salad. Serves 2.
■ Use thinly sliced prosciutto if you prefer.
note – accompany this with the roast garlic mash on page 134 of the short top + sides chapter.

salt and five spice chicken

2 tablespoons lemon juice
1 tablespoon chilli oil*
pinch Chinese five spice powder*
400g (14 oz) chicken pieces
1 tablespoon sea salt
1 teaspoon five spice powder*, extra

Place the lemon juice, chilli oil and the pinch of five spice powder in a bowl and combine. Add the chicken, stir to coat and allow to stand for 5 minutes.
Preheat the oven to 200°C (400°F). Place a large frying pan over high heat. Add the chicken pieces, skin-side down, and cook for 2 minutes each side or until crisp and golden. Transfer to a baking tray and bake for 8–10 minutes or until cooked through.
Combine the salt and extra five spice powder. To serve, place the chicken and small piles of the salt and spice mixture on plates. Serve rice and greens on the side. To eat, dip the chicken pieces into the salt and spice mixture. Serves 2.

salt and five spice chicken

sweet chilli prawn cakes

grilled tomato bruschetta salad

coconut and salmon laksa

sweet chilli prawn cakes

600g (1¼ lb) green (raw) prawn (shrimp) meat
1 egg white
2 kaffir lime* leaves, shredded
3 tablespoons sweet chilli sauce
2 cups fresh breadcrumbs
3 tablespoons rice flour
oil for shallow-frying
sweet chilli sauce, extra, to serve

Process the prawn meat, egg white, kaffir lime leaves, sweet chilli sauce, breadcrumbs and rice flour in a food processor until the mixture is combined but not smooth. With wetted hands, shape the mixture into small cakes. Heat enough oil in a frying pan over medium-high heat to shallow-fry. Add the prawn cakes a few at a time and cook for 3 minutes each side or until golden. Drain on paper towel and serve with extra sweet chilli sauce and salad greens. Serves 4.
note – these prawn cakes are a great small bite to serve with drinks. Shape the cakes and refrigerate, then shallow-fry them just before serving.

grilled tomato bruschetta salad

2 tomatoes, halved
4 slices crusty Italian bread
cracked black pepper
olive oil
1 clove garlic, halved
50g (1¾ oz) rocket (arugula) leaves
50g (1¾ oz) baby English spinach leaves
balsamic vinegar and olive oil for a dressing
shaved parmesan cheese to serve

Place the tomatoes and bread on a tray, sprinkle with pepper and drizzle with oil. Place under a preheated hot grill (broiler). Cook the bread for 1 minute, turn and cook for a further minute or until golden. Remove the bread and continue cooking the tomatoes for a further 10 minutes or until soft. Rub both sides of the bread with the garlic clove. Place the rocket and spinach leaves on plates and top with the bruschetta and tomatoes. Sprinkle over some combined balsamic vinegar and olive oil, then top with parmesan cheese. Serves 2.
note – you can omit the bruschetta from this recipe and place the tomato, rocket and spinach salad in the parmesan shortcrust pastry shell on page 173 of the basics chapter.

coconut and salmon laksa

150g (5 oz) dry rice vermicelli
4 tablespoons quality laksa paste*
1 tablespoon shredded ginger
1 kaffir lime* leaf, shredded (optional)
3½ cups (28 fl oz) fish or vegetable stock
2 cups (16 fl oz) coconut milk
250g (8 oz) salmon fillet, chopped
4 baby bok choy*, leaves separated
chopped red chillies and coriander (cilantro) leaves to serve

Place the rice noodles in a bowl of boiling water and allow to stand for 2 minutes. Drain and set aside.
Place the laksa paste, ginger and kaffir lime leaf in a saucepan over medium-high heat and cook for 1 minute or until fragrant. Add the stock and coconut milk and reduce the temperature to low.
When the coconut broth is hot, add the salmon and bok choy and cook for 1–2 minutes. Place the rice noodles in the bottom of bowls and ladle the broth, salmon and bok choy over the top. Sprinkle with chopped chillies and coriander leaves. Serves 4.

peppered garfish with lemon rice pilaf

4 garfish, butterflied
oil
sea salt and cracked black pepper
lemon rice pilaf
1 tablespoon oil
1 onion, chopped
1½ cups long-grain rice
3 cups (24 fl oz) vegetable or chicken stock
2–3 tablespoons lemon juice
2 tablespoons chopped flat-leaf parsley
sea salt and cracked black pepper

To cook the pilaf, heat the oil in a saucepan over medium heat. Add the onion and cook for 2 minutes or until soft. Add the rice and cook for 1 minute. Add the stock and cook for 10–12 minutes or until tunnels have formed in the rice and almost all the stock has been absorbed. Stir through the lemon juice, parsley, salt and pepper.
While the pilaf is cooking, brush the garfish with oil. Sprinkle with salt and pepper. Heat a frying pan over high heat and cook the garfish for 2–3 minutes each side or until it has a crisp skin and is cooked through. Serve with the lemon pilaf. Serves 2.

peppered garfish with lemon rice pilaf

spiced chicken with chilli pilaf

2 tablespoons oil

3 red chillies, seeded and chopped

1½ cups rice

3 cups (24 fl oz) chicken stock

150g (5 oz) snake beans, halved

spiced chicken

2 tablespoons oil

4 chicken breast fillets, halved

2 tablespoons ground cumin

2 teaspoons ground cinnamon

cracked black pepper

To make the chilli pilaf, place the oil in a saucepan over medium-high heat. Add the chilli and cook for 1 minute. Add the rice and cook for a further 1 minute. Add the stock and bring to the boil. Reduce the heat and allow the rice to simmer for 10–12 minutes or until almost all the liquid has been absorbed. Place the snake beans on top of the rice, cover tightly and remove from the heat.
While the rice is cooking, make the spiced chicken. Place the oil in a frying pan over medium-high heat. Toss the chicken pieces with the combined cumin, cinnamon and pepper and cook for 2 minutes each side or until golden. To serve, place the snake beans on plates and top with the chilli pilaf and chicken. Serves 4.

grilled fennel salad

4 baby fennel bulbs, halved

150g (5 oz) goat's cheese, sliced

1 tablespoon thyme leaves

olive oil

cracked black pepper

180g (6 oz) baby rocket (arugula) leaves

150g (5 oz) cherry tomatoes, quartered

balsamic vinegar and olive oil to serve

Place the fennel, cut-side up, on a baking tray. Top the fennel with the goat's cheese, thyme and a little olive oil. Place under a preheated hot grill (broiler) for 5 minutes or until the fennel has softened but is still firm.
To serve, place the rocket leaves and tomatoes on plates and top with the grilled fennel and goat's cheese. To serve, drizzle with balsamic vinegar and olive oil. Serve with slices of crusty grain bread. Serves 4.

lemon and parsley fried fish

2 tablespoons finely grated lemon rind

¼ cup chopped flat-leaf parsley

sea salt and cracked black pepper

4 fillets white fish

olive oil

lemon wedges and greens to serve

Combine the lemon rind, parsley, salt and pepper in a bowl. Press the lemon and parsley mixture onto both sides of the fish. Heat a little oil in a large frying pan over high heat. Cook the fish for 1–2 minutes each side or until cooked to your liking. Serve with lemon wedges and steamed greens. Serves 4.

stir-fried beef, ginger and greens

1 tablespoon sesame oil

2 tablespoons shredded ginger

2 cloves garlic, sliced

500g (1 lb) rump steak, sliced

500g (1 lb) Asian greens, trimmed and halved

2 tablespoons oyster sauce

½ cup (4 fl oz) Chinese cooking wine*

2 teaspoons cornflour (cornstarch)

¼ cup sliced garlic chives

Place the oil in a wok or frying pan over high heat. Add the ginger and garlic and cook for 1 minute or until soft. Add the beef and stir-fry for 2–3 minutes or until well browned and sealed. Add the greens, oyster sauce and cooking wine and stir-fry for 2 minutes. Mix the cornflour with a little water to form a smooth paste. Add to the pan and stir-fry for 2 minutes or until the greens are tender and the sauce has thickened. Sprinkle with the garlic chives and serve with rice or rice noodles. Serves 4.

spiced chicken with chilli pilaf

lemon and parsley fried fish

grilled fennel salad

stir-fried beef, ginger and greens

61

veal with tomato and bocconcini   bacon and broad bean soup

chicken simmered in soy and star anise

veal with tomato and bocconcini

1 tablespoon oil
4 veal steaks
4 slices crusty bread
4 small bocconcini*, sliced
2 tomatoes, sliced
olive oil
shredded basil to serve

Place the oil in a frying pan over high heat. Add the veal and cook for 1 minute each side or until sealed. Place the veal and bread on a baking tray, top the veal with the bocconcini and tomato and drizzle both the veal and bread with a little olive oil.
Cook the veal and bread under a preheated hot grill (broiler) for 2–3 minutes or until the bread is toasted and the bocconcini has started to melt. To serve, place a little shredded basil on the bread, top with the veal and a little more basil. Serve with a simple green salad. Serves 4.

bacon and broad bean soup

2 teaspoons oil
2 leeks, chopped
2 tablespoons rosemary leaves
6 rashers bacon, rind removed and sliced
2 x 440g (1 lb) cans peeled tomatoes,
   lightly crushed
1 cup (8 fl oz) red wine
2 cups (16 fl oz) beef stock
1½ cups broad (fava) beans■
sea salt and cracked black pepper

Heat the oil in a large saucepan over medium heat. Add the leek, rosemary and bacon and cook for 5 minutes or until the leek is soft. Add the tomatoes, wine and stock and allow to simmer for 8 minutes. Add the broad beans and cook for 5 minutes or until tender. Season with salt and pepper. Serve the soup with bread. Serves 4.
■ Use frozen broad beans if fresh ones are unavailable.

chicken simmered in soy and star anise

⅓ cup (2¾ fl oz) soy sauce
¼ cup (2 fl oz) Chinese cooking wine* or sherry
2 tablespoons oyster sauce
2 star anise*
1 cinnamon stick
2 tablespoons brown sugar
2 chicken breast fillets
1 bunch bok choy* or other Chinese greens, trimmed
   and halved

Place the soy, cooking wine, oyster sauce, star anise, cinnamon stick and sugar in a frying pan over high heat and bring to the boil. Add the chicken and cook for 3 minutes each side. Add the greens and cook for 2 minutes or until tender.
To serve, place the chicken and greens on plates and spoon over the pan juices. Serve with steamed rice. Serves 2.

pasta with rocket and blue cheese

400g (14 oz) fresh* or dry pasta
2 tablespoons butter
½ cup walnuts
2 tablespoons cider vinegar
3 tablespoons chopped chives
180g (6 oz) baby rocket (arugula) leaves
150g (5 oz) blue cheese, sliced
cracked black pepper

Place the pasta in a saucepan of boiling salted water and cook until al dente.
While the pasta is cooking, heat the butter in a small frying pan over medium heat. Add the walnuts and cook for 2 minutes or until fragrant. Add the cider vinegar.
Drain the pasta and toss with the chives, rocket, blue cheese, walnut dressing and pepper.
Serve the pasta with bread and a tomato salad in a simple balsamic dressing. Serves 4.

pasta with rocket and blue cheese

parmesan crusted chicken

grilled eggplant with basil salsa verde

garlic beef with spiced couscous

chicken poached in coconut curry

parmesan crusted chicken

2 chicken breast fillets
2 egg whites, lightly beaten
1 cup grated parmesan cheese
cracked black pepper
2 tablespoons oil
2 ripe tomatoes, sliced
2 tablespoons shredded basil
balsamic vinegar and olive oil to serve

Cut each chicken fillet into two thin, flat pieces. Dip each piece in the egg white and then press into the combined parmesan and pepper.
Place the oil in a non-stick frying pan over medium-high heat. Add the chicken pieces and cook for 1–2 minutes each side or until golden and cooked through, allowing the parmesan crust to brown and crisp before trying to turn over.
To serve, place the tomato and basil on plates. Sprinkle over some balsamic vinegar and olive oil and top with the slices of chicken. Serve with lemon wedges and bread. Serves 2.

garlic beef with spiced couscous

1 tablespoon oil
3 cloves garlic, sliced
2 sirloin steaks
spiced couscous
1 cup couscous
1½ cups (12 fl oz) chicken stock, boiling
2 tablespoons butter
2 teaspoons cumin seeds
2 tablespoons chopped coriander (cilantro)
sea salt and cracked black pepper

To make the spiced couscous, place the couscous and stock in a bowl. Cover tightly with plastic wrap and allow to stand for 4–5 minutes or until the stock has been absorbed. While the couscous is standing, place the butter in a frying pan over medium heat. Add the cumin seeds and cook for 2 minutes. Add the couscous, coriander, salt and pepper and cook for 1 minute or until heated through.
To cook the steak, place the oil in a frying pan over high heat. Press the garlic slices into the steaks and place in the hot pan. Cook for 2 minutes each side or to your liking.
To serve, place the couscous on plates and top with the steak. Serve with steamed greens. Serves 2.

grilled eggplant with basil salsa verde

2 eggplants (aubergines), halved
4 tomatoes, halved
basil salsa verde
⅓ cup chopped flat-leaf parsley
⅔ cup chopped basil
2 cloves garlic, sliced
1 tablespoon Dijon mustard
3 tablespoons salted capers, rinsed
⅓ cup (2¾ fl oz) olive oil
2 tablespoons lemon juice

Cut deep slits in the eggplants and tomatoes and place on a baking tray.
To make the basil salsa verde, process the parsley, basil, garlic, mustard and capers in a food processor or blender until finely chopped. Add the oil and lemon juice and process until a smooth paste forms.
Spread the basil salsa verde over the eggplant and tomatoes. Place under a preheated hot grill (broiler) and cook for 5 minutes or until the eggplant is soft. Serve with grilled flatbreads and firm goat's cheese. Serves 4.

chicken poached in coconut curry

3 tablespoons red curry paste*
6 chicken thigh fillets, halved
2 cups chopped orange sweet potato (kumara)
2 cups (16 fl oz) chicken stock
1½ cups (12 fl oz) coconut milk
¼ cup coriander (cilantro) leaves

Place the curry paste in a frying pan over medium-high heat and cook for 1–2 minutes or until fragrant. Add the chicken and sweet potato to the pan and cook for 2 minutes. Add the stock and coconut milk and reduce the heat to low.■
Allow to simmer gently for 12 minutes or until the chicken and sweet potato are cooked.
To serve, sprinkle the coriander over the chicken. Serve with steamed rice or steamed greens. Serves 4.
■ Do not boil the coconut milk as it will separate—the flavour will be the same but the appearance and texture of the sauce will be different.

Hokkien noodles with sesame chicken

400g (14 oz) fresh Hokkien noodles*
2 teaspoons sesame oil
2 onions, chopped
3–4 chicken breast fillets, sliced
3 tablespoons soy sauce
1/2 cup (4 fl oz) Chinese cooking wine* or dry sherry
2 tablespoons white miso paste*
2 cups greens, such as spinach or bok choy*
1 tablespoon sesame seeds

Wash the noodles under hot water to separate, then drain and set aside. Place the oil in a frying pan or wok over high heat. Add the onion and cook for 2 minutes. Add the chicken and cook for 4 minutes or until well browned. Add the soy, wine, miso, greens and noodles and cook for 4 minutes or until the greens are tender. To serve, place in bowls and sprinkle with sesame seeds. Serves 4.

kaffir lime leaf and chilli lentils

1 tablespoon oil
4 medium red chillies, chopped
2 tablespoons shredded ginger
5 kaffir lime* leaves, shredded
1 1/2 cups red lentils
3 cups (24 fl oz) vegetable or chicken stock
1 cup Thai basil* leaves
1/2 cup coriander (cilantro) leaves
steamed snake beans to serve

Place the oil in a frying pan over medium heat. Add the chillies, ginger and kaffir lime leaves and cook for 1 minute. Add the lentils and stock and cook for 5–6 minutes or until the lentils are cooked but firm.
To serve, place the Thai basil and coriander in bowls and top with the lentils. Serve with steamed snake beans. Serves 4.

pork cutlets with ginger sweet potato mash

2 pork cutlets
sesame seeds
1 tablespoon oil
ginger sweet potato mash
400g (14 oz) orange sweet potato (kumara), peeled and chopped
2 tablespoons shredded ginger
30g (1 oz) butter
1 tablespoon honey
milk
2 tablespoons coriander (cilantro) leaves

To make the mash, place the sweet potato and ginger in a saucepan of boiling water and cook for 5–7 minutes or until tender. Drain. Mash the sweet potato with the butter, honey and enough milk to make it smooth. Stir the coriander through the mash.
While the sweet potato is cooking, press the pork cutlets in the sesame seeds to coat each side. Place the oil in a frying pan over medium heat. Add the pork and cook for 2–3 minutes each side or until golden and cooked to your liking. Serve with the mash and steamed greens. Serves 2.
note – this is great served with the asparagus with balsamic butter on page 134 of the short top + sides chapter.

salad of lamb noodles and peanuts

200g (6 1/2 oz) dry cellophane (beanthread) noodles*
1 tablespoon chilli oil*
1 clove garlic, chopped
500g (1 lb) tender lamb strips
150g (5 oz) snow peas (mange tout), shredded
1/2 red capsicum (bell pepper), sliced
3 tablespoons soy sauce
2 tablespoons sweet chilli sauce
1/4 cup coriander (cilantro) leaves
1/2 cup roasted unsalted peanuts, roughly chopped

Place the noodles in a bowl and cover with boiling water. Allow to stand for 4 minutes or until soft. Drain.
Place the chilli oil in a wok or frying pan over high heat. Add the garlic and cook for 30 seconds. Add the lamb and stir-fry for 3 minutes or until sealed. Add the snow peas and capsicum and stir-fry for 2 minutes. Add the soy and sweet chilli sauces and remove from the heat. Toss through the noodles, coriander leaves and peanuts. Place in bowls and serve with wedges of lime. Serves 4.

Hokkien noodles with sesame chicken

pork cutlets with ginger sweet potato mash

kaffir lime leaf and chilli lentils

salad of lamb noodles and peanuts

soy quail stir-fry   figs baked on haloumi

warmed olive and garlic pasta

soy quail stir-fry

2 teaspoons sesame oil
4 quails, quartered
1/3 cup (2¾ fl oz) salt-reduced soy sauce
1/3 cup (2¾ fl oz) Chinese cooking wine* or dry sherry
2 tablespoons oyster sauce
2 tablespoons brown sugar
6 green onions (scallions), sliced
150g (5 oz) shiitake mushrooms*, sliced
150g (5 oz) snow peas (mange tout), halved
noodles to serve

Place the oil in a wok or frying pan over high heat. Add the quail and stir-fry for 5 minutes or until well browned. Add the soy, wine, oyster sauce and sugar and cook for 2–3 minutes or until the sauce has reduced by half. Add the onions, mushrooms and snow peas and cook for 2 minutes or until tender. Serve the quail on stir-fried hot noodles. Serves 4.

figs baked on haloumi

8 figs, halved
4 long slices prosciutto*, halved lengthwise
60g (2 oz) butter, softened
cracked black pepper
8 slices haloumi*

Preheat the oven to 220°C (425°F). Wrap each fig with prosciutto, place a little butter on the top of each fig and sprinkle with pepper.
Place the haloumi on a baking tray and top each slice with two wrapped figs. Bake for 12 minutes or until the prosciutto is crisp and the figs are soft. Place on a serving plate and serve with a green salad. Serves 4.
note – you can also adapt this recipe to a tart. Place the haloumi and wrapped figs, uncooked, in a blind-baked shortcrust pastry shell (see page 170 of the basics chapter) and then bake for 12 minutes in the pastry shell.

warmed olive and garlic pasta

400g (14 oz) fresh* or dry pasta
2 tablespoons olive oil
1 cup fresh breadcrumbs
1 tablespoon olive oil, extra
3 cloves garlic, sliced
2 tablespoons rosemary leaves
2 teaspoons shredded lemon rind
1 cup olives of your choice
cracked black pepper

Place the pasta in a saucepan of boiling salted water and cook for 4–5 minutes (for fresh pasta) or 8–12 minutes (for dried pasta) or until al dente. Drain.
While the pasta is cooking, place the oil in a frying pan over high heat. Add the breadcrumbs and toast them, stirring, for 2–3 minutes or until golden. Set aside. Wipe the pan clean and heat the extra oil. Add the garlic and cook for 1 minute or until lightly golden. Add the rosemary, lemon, olives and pepper and cook for 2–3 minutes or until warmed through.
To serve, toss the olive mixture through the warm pasta and top with the toasted breadcrumbs. Serve with a green salad. Serves 4.
note – instead of topping with toasted breadcrumbs, serve with the sesame sweet potato on page 134 of the short top + sides chapter as shown in the cover photograph.

basil frittata with gravlax

4 eggs, lightly beaten
1/2 cup (4 fl oz) milk
1/3 cup shredded basil
1/3 cup grated aged cheddar cheese
cracked black pepper
6–8 slices gravlax*

Place the eggs, milk, basil, cheddar and pepper in a bowl and mix to combine. Pour the mixture into a non-stick 20cm (8 in) frying pan and cook over medium heat for 4 minutes or until the frittata is almost set. Place under a hot grill (broiler) for 1 minute or until golden. Remove from the pan and cut into wedges. To serve, top with the gravlax. Serves 2.

basil frittata with gravlax

barbecue pork san choy bau

2 teaspoons sesame oil
2 tablespoons shredded ginger
4 green onions (scallions), sliced
500g (1 lb) Chinese barbecue pork*, sliced
2 tablespoons hoisin sauce*
2 tablespoons soy sauce
beansprouts
iceberg lettuce cups
extra hoisin sauce to serve

Place the oil in a frying pan or wok over medium-high heat. Add the ginger and onions and cook for 1 minute. Add the pork, and hoisin and soy sauces and cook for 3 minutes or until heated through.
To serve, place a small pile of beansprouts in each lettuce leaf. Top with the pork mixture and serve with extra hoisin sauce. Serves 4.

warm pork and fennel salad

1 tablespoon oil
650g (1 lb 5 oz) pork fillet, trimmed
4 small fennel bulbs, sliced
1 cup (8 fl oz) dry white wine
cracked black pepper
2 tablespoons rosemary leaves
125g (4 oz) baby English spinach leaves

Place the oil in a frying pan over medium heat. Add the pork and cook for 2 minutes each side or until well browned and sealed. Remove the pork and set aside.
Add the fennel, wine, pepper and rosemary to the pan. Cover and cook for 6 minutes. Place the pork on top of the fennel and cook, covered, for a further 6 minutes or until the pork is cooked to your liking. To serve, slice the pork and place on plates with the fennel and pan juices, and the baby spinach leaves on the side. Serves 4.

harissa fried fish with warm coriander potatoes

4 x 150g (5 oz) fillets or pieces white fish, such as blue-eye
   cod or swordfish
2–3 tablespoons harissa*
1 tablespoon oil
warm coriander potatoes
500g (1 lb) boiling potatoes, such as kipfler
2 cloves garlic, crushed
1/2 cup thick plain yoghurt
2 tablespoons chopped mint
2 tablespoons chopped coriander (cilantro)
sea salt and cracked black pepper

To make the warm coriander potatoes, halve the potatoes, place them in a saucepan of boiling water and cook for 15 minutes or until soft. Drain and allow to cool slightly. While the potatoes are cooking, spread the fish with the harissa. Place the oil in a non-stick frying pan over medium-high heat. Add the fish and cook for 2–3 minutes each side or to your liking.
Combine the garlic, yoghurt, mint, coriander, salt and pepper and toss through the warm potatoes. Place on a serving plate and top with the harissa fried fish. Serves 4.
note – instead of the warm coriander potatoes, the fish is great served with the roast garlic mash potatoes on page 134 of the short top + sides chapter.

honey lamb kebabs

400g (14 oz) lean lamb loin or fillets
2 tablespoons honey
2 teaspoons grated lemon rind
1 tablespoon rosemary leaves
cracked black pepper
couscous and baby English spinach leaves to serve

Cut the lamb into strips or cubes and thread onto skewers. Combine the honey, lemon rind, rosemary and pepper and spread over the kebabs. Place under a preheated hot grill (broiler) and cook for 1–2 minutes each side or until cooked to your liking. Serve on couscous with baby English spinach. Serves 2.
note – you can also serve these kebabs with the sesame sweet potatoes on page 134 of the short top + sides chapter.

barbecue pork san choy bau

harissa fried fish with warm coriander potatoes

warm pork and fennel salad

honey lamb kebabs

pink apple tarts

caramelised strawberry shortcake

waffles with vanilla espresso syrup

pink apple tarts

2 sheets ready-prepared puff pastry
2 pink lady or sweet red apples
brown sugar

Preheat the oven to 220°C (425°F). Trim 1cm (½ in) from the edges of the pastry and cut each sheet into 2 pieces. Core the apples and slice thinly.
Place the pastry on baking trays lined with non-stick baking paper. Place a layer of apples down the middle of the pastry. Sprinkle the apples with brown sugar. Bake for 12 minutes or until puffed and golden. Serve with thick cream or ice cream. Serves 4.

caramelised strawberry shortcake

500g (1 lb) strawberries
½ cup caster (superfine) sugar
4 good-quality shortbread biscuits
thick cream or ice cream to serve

Remove the stalks from the strawberries and wash and drain. Place the sugar on a plate and roll the strawberries in the sugar to coat lightly.
Place the strawberries in a non-stick frying pan over high heat and cook for 2 minutes or until they are warm and the sugar is dissolved. Remove the strawberries from the pan and set aside. Cook the remaining syrup for 2 minutes.
To serve, place the shortbread on serving plates, top with the warm strawberries and pour over the warm strawberry sauce. Serve immediately with thick cream or ice cream. Serves 4.

waffles with vanilla espresso syrup

8 waffles
thick cream or ice cream to serve
vanilla espresso syrup
1 cup (8 fl oz) freshly brewed strong espresso
¾ cup caster (superfine) sugar
2 teaspoons vanilla extract

To make the syrup, place the espresso, sugar and vanilla in a saucepan over low heat and stir until the sugar is dissolved. Increase the heat and simmer rapidly for 8 minutes or until the liquid is syrupy.
To serve, warm or toast the waffles and place on serving plates. Pour the vanilla espresso syrup over them and serve with thick cream or vanilla bean or espresso ice cream. Serves 4.

little chocolate brownies

150g (5 oz) butter, softened
1 cup caster (superfine) sugar
¾ cup cocoa powder
2 eggs
1 cup plain (all-purpose) flour
1 teaspoon baking powder

Preheat the oven to 180°C (350°F). Place the butter and sugar in a bowl and beat until light and fluffy. Add the cocoa, eggs, flour and baking powder and mix until combined. Spoon the mixture into nine ½ cup (4 fl oz) capacity non-stick muffin tins. Bake for 10–12 minutes or until the cakes are cooked but still soft in the centre. To serve, invert the cakes onto plates. Serve warm with thick cream or ice cream and espresso coffee. Makes 9 cakes.

little chocolate brownies

coconut poached pears

2 cups (16 fl oz) coconut milk
1/3 cup sugar
1 cinnamon stick
4 small soft pears, peeled and halved

Place the coconut milk, sugar and cinnamon in a saucepan over medium-low heat. Do not let the coconut milk boil as it will separate. Add the pears and cook for 15 minutes, turning once. To serve, place the pears in bowls and serve warm with the coconut broth. Serves 4.

vanilla simmered quince

2 cups (16 fl oz) water
1 cup sugar
1 vanilla bean*, split
1 quince, peeled and sliced

Place the water, sugar and vanilla bean in a frying pan over high heat and stir until the sugar is dissolved. Add the quince to the pan, cover and simmer for 12 minutes or until tender. To serve, place the quinces in bowls and pour over some of the simmering liquid. Serves 2.

chocolate and hazelnut pastries

1 sheet ready-prepared puff pastry
1/4 cup chopped dark chocolate
1/2 teaspoon ground cinnamon
2 tablespoons chopped roasted hazelnuts

Preheat the oven to 200°C (400°F). Trim the edges of the pastry and cut the sheet into 4 long pieces. Cover half of each piece with the chocolate and sprinkle with cinnamon and hazelnuts, leaving a 1cm (1/2 in) border.
Fold over the pastry to enclose and place on a baking tray. Bake for 15 minutes or until puffed and golden. Serve warm or cold. Serves 4.

steamed coconut custards

3/4 cup (6 fl oz) coconut milk
11/4 cups (10 fl oz) cream (single or pouring)
3 tablespoons caster (superfine) sugar
4 egg yolks
1 teaspoon finely grated lime rind

Place the coconut milk, cream, sugar and egg yolks in a bowl and whisk to combine. Stir the lime rind through. Pour the mixture into 4 ramekins* or Chinese tea cups and place in a bamboo steamer*. Steam over boiling water for 6–8 minutes or until the custard is just beginning to set. Allow to stand for 5 minutes before serving. Serves 4.

coconut poached pears

chocolate and hazelnut pastries

vanilla simmered quince

steamed coconut custards

30

minutes

risotto

pizza

tempura

rice paper rolls

soup

rosti

soft polenta

corn cakes

salsa verde

steamed chicken

star anise duck salad

sesame beef rice paper rolls

angel hair niçoise

star anise duck salad

4 duck breasts, trimmed of fat
1/3 cup (2¾ fl oz) red wine
1/3 cup (2¾ fl oz) chicken stock
2 star anise*
6 green onions (scallions), sliced
175g (6 oz) mizuna or Asian salad greens

Place the duck breasts, skin-side down, in a preheated frying pan over high heat and cook for 10 minutes or until the skin is well browned and crisp. Remove the duck from the pan and set aside. Drain off the fat from the pan. Add the red wine, stock and star anise and cook for 5 minutes or until the liquid has reduced by half. Return the duck to the pan, uncooked-side down, and allow to rest in the pan over medium heat for 4 minutes.
Combine the onions and mizuna or greens and place on plates. To serve, slice the duck, place on top of the greens and pour over the pan juices. Serves 4.

sesame beef rice paper rolls

1 tablespoon oil
400g (14 oz) rump steak
1 tablespoon sesame oil
1 tablespoon soy sauce
2 bunches English spinach, leaves only
2 tablespoons sesame seeds
12 rice paper rounds*
100g (3½ oz) snow pea (mange tout) sprouts
soy sauce for dipping

Place the oil in a frying pan over high heat. Add the steak and cook for 2–3 minutes each side or to your liking. Set aside for 2 minutes then slice the steak thinly and place in a bowl with the sesame oil and soy.
Place the spinach leaves in a saucepan of boiling water and cook for 5 seconds. Drain and squeeze any excess liquid from the spinach. Roughly chop and combine with the sesame seeds.
Dip the rice paper rounds in hot water for 5–10 seconds or until soft. Remove and pat dry. Place the beef, spinach and snow pea sprouts down the centre of the rice paper rounds. Fold one end over the filling to form a base then roll in the sides to enclose. Repeat with the remaining mixture. Serve with the soy sauce. Serves 4.

angel hair niçoise

400g (14 oz) fresh angel hair pasta*
2 tablespoons chilli oil*
350g (11 oz) tuna steaks
3 tablespoons lime juice
2 tablespoons olive oil
1 clove garlic, crushed
6 anchovy fillets, chopped
200g (6½ oz) green beans, blanched*
¾ cup olives
¼ cup roughly chopped flat-leaf parsley

Place the pasta in a large saucepan of boiling salted water over high heat and cook until al dente.
While the pasta is cooking, place a frying pan over high heat. Add the chilli oil and tuna steaks and sear the tuna for 1 minute each side. Remove the tuna from the pan and slice into pieces. Reduce the pan heat to low, add the lime juice, olive oil, garlic and anchovies and cook for 1 minute. Drain the pasta and place in a bowl with the tuna, beans, olives and parsley. Pour the warm dressing from the pan over the pasta and toss to combine. Serves 4.

lentil and pancetta soup

1 tablespoon oil
2 leeks, chopped
8 slices pancetta*, chopped
400g (14 oz) brown lentils
6 cups (48 fl oz) chicken or vegetable stock
extra pancetta*
sea salt and cracked black pepper

Place the oil in a saucepan over medium heat. Add the leeks and pancetta and cook for 3 minutes. Add the lentils and stock and bring to the boil. Allow the soup to boil rapidly for 15–18 minutes or until the lentils are soft.
While the soup is cooking, place a few slices of the extra pancetta under a hot grill (broiler) and cook for 1 minute each side or until crisp.
To serve, season the soup with salt and pepper and ladle into bowls. Top with the crisp pancetta and serve with lemon wedges to be squeezed over the soup, or a spoonful of crème fraîche. Serves 4.
note – for something a little different, serve the soup with the plain garlic bruschetta on page 126 of the short top + sides chapter.

lentil and pancetta soup

rocket, chicken and pine nut tabouli

fried bug-tails on garlic spinach

chickens baked with quince paste and prosciutto

rocket, chicken and pine nut tabouli

3/4 cup burghul (cracked wheat)
1 1/2 cups (12 fl oz) boiling water
1 tablespoon oil
3 chicken breast fillets
250g (8 oz) rocket (arugula) leaves
3/4 cup flat-leaf parsley, chopped
3/4 cup mint, chopped
200g (6 1/2 oz) cherry tomatoes, quartered
1/2 cup pine nuts, toasted
3 tablespoons lemon juice
3 tablespoons olive oil
sea salt and cracked black pepper
lemon wedges to serve

Combine the burghul and boiling water in a bowl. Allow to stand for 5 minutes or until the burghul has absorbed all the water and is soft.
Place the oil in a frying pan over medium-high heat. Add the chicken and cook for 5 minutes each side or until cooked through. Set aside to cool.
Place the burghul, rocket, parsley, mint, tomatoes and pine nuts in a bowl. Slice the chicken and add to the salad. Combine the lemon juice, olive oil, salt and pepper. Pour over the salad and toss to combine. To serve, place on plates with lemon wedges. Serves 4.

fried bug-tails on garlic spinach

4 green (raw) Balmain or Moreton Bay bug-tails*
rice flour
oil for shallow-frying
1/4 cup sage leaves
garlic spinach
2 bunches (650g or 1 lb 5 oz) English spinach
75g (2 1/2 oz) butter
2–3 cloves garlic, chopped
lemon wedges to serve

To make the garlic spinach, plunge the leaves in a saucepan of boiling water for 3 seconds. Drain and squeeze out the excess liquid. Set aside.
Remove the bug meat in one piece from the shell. Toss lightly in rice flour and shake away any excess. Place a frying pan over medium-high heat with enough oil to shallow-fry. Add the bug-tails and cook for 1–2 minutes each side or until golden and crisp. Drain on paper towel. Add the sage to the oil and cook for 1 minute or until crisp. Drain.
Place the butter and garlic in a frying pan over medium heat and cook for 1 minute. Add the spinach and toss to coat. To serve, place on plates, top with the bug-tails and sage and serve with lemon wedges. Serves 4.

chickens baked with quince paste and prosciutto

4 bay leaves
2 teaspoons fennel seeds
4 x 300g (10 oz) small poussins (baby chickens)
30g (1 oz) quince paste*
16 slices prosciutto*
4 leeks, halved
olive oil
sea salt and cracked black pepper
1 cup (8 fl oz) dry white wine

Preheat the oven to 240°C (475°F). Place a bay leaf and some fennel seeds in the cavity of each chicken. Tie the legs with string to secure. Spread some of the quince paste on the breast of the chickens. Wrap the prosciutto slices around the chickens and tuck under to secure.
Place the leeks in the base of a baking dish, drizzle with a little olive oil and sprinkle with salt and pepper. Pour the wine into the base of the baking dish and place the chickens on top of the leeks. Bake for 20 minutes or until the chickens are cooked through. Serve with the roasted leeks and steamed greens or a green salad. Serves 4.

rare tuna spring rolls with lime and soy

500g (1 lb) piece sashimi tuna*
1 tablespoon wasabi paste*
2 tablespoons coriander (cilantro) leaves
2 tablespoons chopped flat-leaf parsley
8 spring roll wrappers■
oil for deep-frying
2 tablespoons lime juice
2 tablespoons soy sauce

To make the spring rolls, cut the tuna into pieces 2cm (3/4 in) wide and 10cm (4 in) long. Spread each piece of tuna very lightly with the wasabi paste and roll the tuna in the coriander and parsley. Wrap each piece of tuna in a spring roll wrapper and use a little water to seal the ends.
Deep-fry the spring rolls in hot oil for 30–45 seconds or until lightly golden. Drain on paper towel. Combine the lime juice and soy and place in small dipping bowls. To serve, place the tuna rolls on plates with a bowl of dipping sauce. Serve with a salad of Asian greens. Serves 4.
■ Available from Asian food stores.

rare tuna spring rolls with lime and soy

eggplant with tomato, basil and parmesan risotto

spiced lamb fillets with onion couscous

chicken baked on sweet potato rosti

white wine risotto with field mushrooms

egglant with tomato, basil and parmesan risotto

2 small young eggplants (aubergines)
olive oil
risotto
2¹/₂ cups (20 fl oz) vegetable or chicken stock
2 cups (16 fl oz) tomato puree
1 cup (8 fl oz) quality red wine
1 tablespoon oil
2 cups arborio (risotto) rice*
¹/₃ cup shredded basil
¹/₃ cup grated parmesan cheese
cracked black pepper

To make the risotto, place the stock, tomato puree and wine in a saucepan over medium heat and allow to simmer. Heat the oil in a separate saucepan over medium-high heat. Add the rice and cook for 1 minute or until translucent. Add the hot stock mixture, 1 cup (8 fl oz) at a time, stirring after each cup has been added and absorbed into the rice. Continue adding the stock until the rice is tender and the risotto is creamy.
While the risotto is cooking, slice the eggplants and brush well with oil. Place in a preheated frying pan over high heat and cook for 2 minutes on each side or until golden. Set aside and keep warm.
To serve, stir the basil, parmesan and pepper through the risotto. Place the eggplant slices on serving plates and top with the risotto. Serve with a spoonful of creamy goat's curd or mascarpone on the side. Serves 4.

chicken baked on sweet potato rosti

4 chicken breast fillets, skin on
sea salt and cracked black pepper
sweet potato rosti
550g (1 lb 2 oz) orange sweet potatoes (kumara), peeled
2 tablespoons oil
1 clove garlic, crushed
¹/₂ cup grated parmesan cheese
cracked black pepper

Preheat the oven to 220°C (425°F). To make the sweet potato rosti, cut the sweet potato into thin strips using a sharp vegetable peeler. Toss the sweet potato with oil, garlic, parmesan and pepper. Place on a baking tray lined with non-stick baking paper and bake for 15 minutes. While the sweet potato is cooking, rub salt and pepper into the skin of the chicken. Place a frying pan over high heat and cook, skin-side down, for 4 minutes. Turn and cook for another minute. Place the chicken on top of the rosti and bake for a further 5 minutes or until the chicken is cooked and the sweet potato rosti is crisp and golden brown. Serve with steamed greens. Serves 4.

spiced lamb fillets with onion couscous

1 cup couscous
1¹/₄ cups (10 fl oz) boiling vegetable or chicken stock
2 tablespoons oil
2 onions, sliced
1 tablespoon thyme leaves
spiced lamb
1 tablespoon ground cumin
1 teaspoon ground chilli
1 tablespoon paprika
500g (1 lb) lamb fillets, trimmed
1 tablespoon oil

Place the couscous and boiling stock in a bowl, cover with plastic wrap and allow to stand for 5 minutes or until all the liquid is absorbed. Place the oil in a frying pan over medium heat. Add the onion and thyme and cook for 5–7 minutes or until well browned. Set aside.
To make the spiced lamb, combine the cumin, chilli and paprika in a bowl. Add the lamb fillets and toss to coat. Place the oil in a frying pan over medium-high heat. Add the lamb and cook for 1¹/₂–2 minutes each side or to your liking. Place the couscous in the pan with the onions and warm through. To serve, slice the lamb and place on plates on top of the couscous and some rocket (arugula). Serves 4.

white wine risotto with field mushrooms

4 large field mushrooms
oil
cracked black pepper
white wine risotto
4 cups (32 fl oz) vegetable or chicken stock
1¹/₂ cups (12 fl oz) quality white wine
2 tablespoons oil
1 leek, chopped
2 cups arborio (risotto) rice*
3 tablespoons lemon juice
¹/₃ cup shredded basil
¹/₂ cup grated parmesan cheese

To make the risotto, place the stock and wine in a saucepan over medium heat and allow to simmer rapidly.
Place the oil in a separate saucepan over medium heat. Add the leek and rice and cook for 2 minutes. Add the stock mixture, a few cups at a time, stirring frequently until the stock has been absorbed. Continue adding stock and stirring until it is all used and the rice is al dente and creamy. While the risotto is cooking, brush the mushrooms with oil and sprinkle with pepper. Place under a preheated hot grill (broiler) and cook for 5 minutes or until soft. To serve, stir the lemon juice, basil and parmesan through the risotto and place in serving bowls. Top with a mushroom and serve. Serves 4.

spinach and ricotta pies

250g (8 oz) baby English spinach leaves
300g (10 oz) ricotta cheese
1 egg
1/4 cup grated parmesan cheese
2 tablespoons chopped dill
cracked black pepper
2 sheets ready-prepared puff pastry

Preheat the oven to 220°C (425°F). Place the spinach in a saucepan of boiling water for 5 seconds. Drain and run under cold water. Squeeze away any excess liquid, roughly chop the spinach and mix with the ricotta, egg, parmesan, dill and pepper.
Cut each pastry sheet in half. Place the filling on one half of each piece and fold over, pressing the edges together to enclose the filling.
Place on a baking tray lined with non-stick baking paper and bake for 15 minutes or until puffed and golden. Serve with a leaf salad. Serves 4.
note – serve with the roast tomato salad on page 134 of the short top + sides chapter.

pumpkin and fetta risotto

500g (1 lb) sweet pumpkin, such as jap or butternut, peeled
   and chopped
oil
sea salt and cracked black pepper
fetta risotto
5½ cups (44 fl oz) chicken or vegetable stock
1 tablespoon oil
2 cups arborio (risotto) rice*
1/4 cup chopped chives
1/4 cup grated parmesan cheese
cracked black pepper
150g (5 oz) marinated fetta cheese in oil

Preheat the oven to 220°C (425°F). Place the pumpkin on a baking tray and toss with oil, salt and pepper. Bake for 20 minutes or until soft.
To cook the risotto, place the stock in a saucepan over medium heat and allow to simmer. Place the oil in a separate saucepan over medium heat. Add the rice and cook for 1 minute or until translucent. Add the stock, 1 cup (8 fl oz) at a time, and stir until absorbed. Continue until all the stock has been used and the rice is creamy. To serve, stir the chives, parmesan, pepper and pumpkin through the risotto. Top with the fetta and its oil. Serves 4.
note – serve with the iceberg salad on page 134 of the short top + sides chapter.

chicken baked in olives, lemon and capers

200g (6½ oz) cherry tomatoes, halved
1/3 cup small Ligurian olives
2 teaspoons grated lemon rind
2 tablespoons salted capers, rinsed
2 tablespoons olive oil
sea salt and cracked black pepper
2 chicken breast fillets

Preheat the oven to 220°C (425°F). Combine the cherry tomatoes, olives, lemon rind, capers, oil, salt and pepper and place in the base of a baking dish.
Place the chicken on top and spoon a little of the olive mixture over to coat. Bake, turning the chicken once, for 20 minutes or until the chicken is cooked.
Serve with boiled potatoes with butter and salt, or greens. Serves 2.

crispy skin rainbow trout with celeriac mash

2 tablespoons sea salt flakes
2 teaspoons cracked black pepper
2 teaspoons juniper berries*, finely chopped
2 tablespoons oil
4 small rainbow (river) trout, gutted and scaled
celeriac mash
3 boiling potatoes, peeled and chopped
1 x 250g (8 oz) celeriac (celery root), peeled and chopped
milk
60g (2 oz) butter
sea salt

To make the celeriac mash, place the potatoes and celeriac in a saucepan and cover with milk. Place the saucepan over medium-high heat and allow to boil gently for 8 minutes or until the potatoes and celeriac are soft.
While the mash is cooking, combine the sea salt flakes, pepper and juniper berries and rub into the skin of the trout. Place the oil in a frying pan over high heat. Add the fish and cook for 4–5 minutes each side or until the skin is crisp and the flesh is tender.
To finish the mash, strain and reserve the hot milk. Add the butter and salt to the vegetables and mash with some of the cooking milk until smooth.
To serve, place the mash onto plates and top with the trout. Serve with lemon wedges and a simple green side salad. Serves 4.

spinach and ricotta pies

pumpkin and fetta risotto

chicken baked in olives, lemon and capers

crispy skin rainbow trout with celeriac mash

seared scallops on lemon and spinach risotto

double-cooked pork ribs

pork steaks with brown sugar apples

seared scallops on lemon and spinach risotto

1 tablespoon oil
sea salt and cracked black pepper
16 scallops, removed from the shell
lemon and spinach risotto
5 1/2 cups (44 fl oz) vegetable stock
2 tablespoons oil
2 cups arborio (risotto) rice*
sea salt and cracked black pepper
2 teaspoons lemon rind, grated
200g (6 1/2 oz) baby English spinach leaves
shaved parmesan cheese to serve

To make the risotto, place the stock in a saucepan over medium-high heat, allow to come to the boil and reduce to a simmer.
Place the oil in another saucepan over medium-high heat. Add the rice and cook for 1 minute. Add the stock, 2 cups (16 fl oz) at a time, stirring frequently and cooking until the stock has been absorbed. Continue adding cups of stock and stirring until all the stock has been absorbed and the rice is tender. Season with salt and pepper and keep the risotto warm.
Place the oil in a frying pan over high heat. Sprinkle salt and pepper over the scallops. Place in the pan and cook for 20–30 seconds each side or until seared.
To serve, stir the lemon rind and spinach leaves through the risotto and spoon onto plates. Top with the scallops and serve with lemon wedges and parmesan on the side. Serves 4.

double-cooked pork ribs

8 pork spare ribs, halved
2 tablespoons soy sauce
3 tablespoons hoisin sauce*
1 tablespoon chilli sauce
1 tablespoon brown sugar

Preheat the oven to 220°C (425°F). Place the pork ribs in the base of a bamboo steamer* and steam over a saucepan of boiling water for 6 minutes.
While the ribs are steaming, combine the soy, hoisin and chilli sauces, and the sugar. Place the ribs on a rack over a baking tray and brush both sides with the sauce. Bake for 10 minutes. Brush the ribs with more sauce, turn and bake for a further 10 minutes. Serve the ribs with steamed greens. Serves 4.
note – for an easy greens with oyster sauce recipe, see page 134 of the short top + sides chapter.

pork steaks with brown sugar apples

4 pork steaks, 1–2cm (1/2–3/4 in) thick
2 tablespoons olive oil
2 tablespoons balsamic vinegar
2 tablespoons chopped sage
brown sugar apples
2 small sweet red apples, sliced
1/3 cup brown sugar
1 tablespoon butter

Place the pork, oil, vinegar and sage in a shallow dish and set aside.
To make the brown sugar apples, press the apple slices into the brown sugar. Place the butter in a large frying pan over medium-high heat and cook the apple slices for 2–3 minutes each side or until golden and soft. Set aside and keep warm.
Place a frying pan over high heat. Drain the pork and cook for 3–5 minutes each side or to your liking. To serve, place the pork on plates with the brown sugar apples and steamed green vegetables. Serves 4.

corn cakes with prosciutto salad

2 cobs corn
1 cup plain (all-purpose) flour
2 eggs
1/4 cup coriander (cilantro), shredded
1 teaspoon ground cumin
2 teaspoons baking powder
pinch sea salt
prosciutto salad
125g (4 oz) baby English spinach or rocket (arugula) leaves
1/2 cup semi-dried tomatoes*, with oil
12 slices prosciutto*
cracked black pepper

Place the corn in a saucepan of boiling water and cook until tender. Remove the corn kernels from the cob. Process the flour, eggs, coriander, cumin, baking powder and salt in a food processor until combined. Add the corn and process until roughly chopped.
Spread 2–3 tablespoons of the mixture in a hot, greased frying pan and cook for 3 minutes each side or until golden. Keep warm and repeat with the remaining mixture.
To serve, place a corn cake on each plate and top with the spinach or rocket, semi-dried tomatoes, prosciutto and pepper. Drizzle over the oil from the semi-dried tomatoes and top with another corn cake. Serve immediately. Serves 4.

corn cakes with prosciutto salad

soft polenta with blue cheese and wine beef

2 cups (16 fl oz) hot water
2 cups (16 fl oz) milk
1 cup quick-cook polenta
60g (2 oz) butter
sea salt and cracked black pepper
150g (5 oz) soft, strong blue cheese
wine beef
1 tablespoon oil
4 fillet steaks
¾ cup (6 fl oz) red wine
¾ cup (6 fl oz) beef stock

Place the water and milk in a saucepan and bring to the boil. Remove from the heat and slowly whisk in the polenta. Return to a low heat and stir for 3 minutes or until the polenta is soft and creamy. Add the butter, salt and pepper, and stir through. Set aside and keep warm.
To make the wine beef, place the oil in a frying pan over medium-high heat. Add the steaks and cook for 3–4 minutes each side or until cooked to your liking. Remove from the pan, cover and keep warm. Add the wine and stock to the pan and boil until reduced by half. To serve, place a large spoonful of polenta on plates and top with the blue cheese. Top with the steak and some pan juices. Serves 4.

Thai chicken salad

1 tablespoon oil
1 tablespoon chopped ginger
1 stalk lemongrass*, chopped
3 red chillies, chopped
500g (1 lb) minced chicken breast
¼ cup (2 fl oz) lemon juice
1 tablespoon fish sauce*
1 red onion, thinly sliced
1 cup coriander (cilantro) leaves
2 tablespoons shredded basil
lettuce leaves to serve

Place the oil in a frying pan over high heat. Add the ginger, lemongrass and chilli and cook for 1 minute. Add the chicken and cook, stirring to break up any lumps, for 5 minutes or until cooked.
Remove the chicken from the heat and allow to cool slightly. Combine the lemon juice and fish sauce. Pour over the chicken. Add the onion, coriander and basil. To serve, place the salad in small bowls and place crisp lettuce leaves on side plates. Serves 4.

salmon baked in salsa verde

4 x 150g (5 oz) pieces salmon fillet
salsa verde
⅓ cup chopped dill
⅓ cup flat-leaf parsley, chopped
⅓ cup mint, chopped
2 cloves garlic, sliced
1 tablespoon Dijon mustard
8 anchovy fillets
3 tablespoons salted capers, rinsed
⅓ cup (2¾ fl oz) olive oil
2 tablespoons lemon juice

Preheat the oven to 200°C (400°F). To make the salsa verde, process the dill, parsley, mint, garlic, mustard, anchovies and capers in a food processor until smooth. Add the oil and lemon juice and process until combined. Place the salmon in a baking dish and spread with the salsa verde. Bake for 6–10 minutes or until the salmon is cooked medium-rare. Serve with steamed greens. Serves 4.

lamb rack with preserved lemon gremolata crust

500g (1 lb) baby new potatoes
sea salt
olive oil
1 lamb rack of 12 cutlets, trimmed of fat
preserved lemon gremolata
2 cloves garlic, crushed
⅔ cup flat-leaf parsley, chopped
1½ tablespoons chopped preserved lemon*
2 tablespoons olive oil

Preheat the oven to 220°C (425°F). Place the potatoes in a baking dish with salt and oil and shake to coat. Bake for 15 minutes.
Place a frying pan over high heat. Add the lamb and cook for 3 minutes or until the meat is sealed. Remove from the pan and set aside.
To make the preserved lemon gremolata, combine the garlic, parsley, preserved lemon and oil. Spread the gremolata over the lamb and place in the baking dish with the potatoes.■ Bake for 12–15 minutes or until the lamb is cooked to your liking.
To serve, place the potatoes on plates. Slice the rack into cutlets, place on the plates and serve with steamed greens. Serves 4.
■ You may need to shield the gremolata from the heat with a little strip of aluminium foil to prevent it from burning, depending on how long you cook the lamb for.

soft polenta with blue cheese and wine beef

salmon baked in salsa verde

Thai chicken salad

lamb rack with preserved lemon gremolata crust

steamed lemongrass chicken and rice rolls

steamed lemongrass chicken and rice rolls

4 stalks lemongrass*, halved lengthwise
3 chicken breast fillets, halved lengthwise
1 tablespoon sesame oil
2 red chillies, seeded and chopped
1 bunch gai larn*, halved
300g (10 oz) plain fresh rice-noodle rolls*
soy sauce to serve

Place the lemongrass in the base of a bamboo steamer*. Place the chicken on top and brush with the sesame oil and sprinkle with the chilli. Place a lid on the steamer, place over a saucepan of boiling water and steam for 3 minutes. While the chicken is steaming, place the gai larn and rice rolls in another bamboo steamer of the same size. Place the noodle steamer on top of the steamer with the chicken and cover. Steam for a further 5 minutes or until the chicken and gai larn are tender. Serve with small bowls of soy sauce and wedges of lime. Serves 4.

tempura fish with chilli salad

2 small fish, such as snapper or coral trout, gutted and scaled
flour to coat
1 quantity tempura batter (see page 165 of basics chapter)
oil for deep-frying
chilli salad
2 large, mild red chillies, seeded and sliced
1/2 Lebanese cucumber, shredded
1/2 red onion, sliced
2 tablespoons chopped coriander (cilantro)
2 tablespoons chopped mint
1 tablespoon lemon juice
1 tablespoon soy sauce

To make the chilli salad, combine the chilli, cucumber, onion, coriander, mint, lemon and soy. Set aside.
To make the tempura fish, coat the fish lightly in flour and shake away any excess. Dip the fish into the batter and place in a wok of hot oil over high or medium-high heat. Cook for 5 minutes each side or until golden and crisp. Drain on paper towel. To serve, place the chilli salad on plates and top with the fish. Serves 4.

parmesan polenta with garlic-grilled vegetables

2 cups (16 fl oz) hot water
2 cups (16 fl oz) milk
1 cup quick-cook polenta
1/3 cup grated parmesan cheese
60g (2 oz) butter
sea salt and cracked black pepper
garlic-grilled vegetables
1/2 cup (4 fl oz) olive oil
3 cloves garlic, chopped
sea salt and cracked black pepper
2 capsicums (bell peppers), halved
2 zucchinis (courgettes), halved
2 radicchio hearts, halved

Place the water and milk in a saucepan and bring to the boil. Remove from the heat and slowly whisk in the polenta. Return to the heat and stir for 3 minutes or until the polenta is soft and creamy. Stir through the parmesan, butter, salt and pepper. Set aside and keep warm.
To make the garlic-grilled vegetables, combine the oil, garlic, salt and pepper. Brush well over the vegetables and place under a preheated hot grill (broiler) and cook for 2–3 minutes each side or until golden. To serve, place the polenta on plates and top with the grilled vegetables. Top with shaved parmesan cheese if desired. Serves 4.

stir-fried pork and shiitake mushrooms

2 teaspoons sesame oil
2 teaspoons oil
2 tablespoons shredded ginger
2 cloves garlic, sliced
500g (1 lb) pork fillet, sliced
cornflour (cornstarch)
200g (6 1/2 oz) fresh shiitake mushrooms*
1/2 cup (4 fl oz) Chinese cooking wine* or sherry
3 tablespoons soy sauce
8 baby bok choy*, leaves separated

Place the oils in a wok or frying pan over high heat. Add the ginger and garlic and cook for 1 minute. Lightly toss the pork in the cornflour and shake away any excess. Add the pork to the pan and cook for 4 minutes or until well sealed. Add the mushrooms, wine, soy and bok choy and stir-fry for 3–4 minutes or until the mushrooms and bok choy are tender. Serve with rice and small bowls of chopped chilli on the side. Serves 4.

tempura fish with chilli salad   parmesan polenta with garlic-grilled vegetables

stir-fried pork and shiitake mushrooms

chicken poached in ginger broth

5 cups (40 fl oz) chicken stock
2 tablespoons shredded ginger
2 coriander (cilantro) roots
350g (11 oz) orange sweet potato (kumara), peeled and sliced
4 chicken breast fillets, halved lengthwise
3 green onions (scallions), sliced

Place the chicken stock, ginger and coriander roots in a deep frying pan over medium-high heat and allow to rapidly simmer for 2 minutes. Add the sweet potato and simmer for 4 minutes. Add the chicken and simmer for a further 5 minutes or until the chicken and sweet potato are soft and tender.
To serve, place the chicken and sweet potato in bowls, spoon over the ginger broth and sprinkle with the onions. Serves 4.

pizza with tomato, olives and rosemary

1 quantity dough (see page 179 of basics chapter)
  or 4 readymade pizza bases
oil
6 bocconcini*, sliced
300g (10 oz) cherry tomatoes, halved
1/3 cup small olives
1/3 cup caper berries*
2 tablespoons rosemary sprigs
12 slices prosciutto* or coppa
cracked black pepper

Preheat the oven to 220°C (425°F). Place two baking trays that will fit the pizzas into the oven to heat. If using fresh dough, divide into 4 pieces and roll out on a lightly floured surface until 2–3mm (1/3 in) thick.
Place the pizza bases on non-stick baking paper and brush well with oil. Top with the bocconcini, tomatoes, olives, caper berries, rosemary, prosciutto and pepper.
Slide the pizzas on the paper onto the hot baking trays and bake for 15 minutes or until the crust is golden. Serve with salad greens. Serves 4.
note – this recipe can also be baked in a tart shell. Place the topping ingredients in a blind-baked pepper and mustard or parmesan shortcrust pastry shell (see page 173 of basics chapter) and bake for 10–15 minutes.

roast beef with sweet pumpkin

8–12 wedges sweet pumpkin, such as jap or butternut
3 parsnips, peeled and halved
2 tablespoons oil
sea salt and cracked black pepper
600g (1 1/4 lb) eye fillet or scotch fillet
1 bunch lemon thyme

Preheat the oven to 220°C (425°F). Place the pumpkin, parsnip, oil, salt and pepper in a baking dish and toss to combine. Bake for 15 minutes while sealing the meat. Place a frying pan over high heat. Add the beef and cook for 1 minute each side or until well browned and sealed. Place the lemon thyme in the base of the baking dish with the pumpkin and rest the fillet on top of the lemon thyme. Return to the oven and cook for 15 minutes or until the meat is cooked to your liking and the pumpkin is soft and golden. Serves 4.

steak sandwiches with roasted garlic

1 tablespoon oil
1 onion, sliced
8 thick slices tomato
8 thin fillet steaks
8 slices bread, toasted
roasted garlic
2 heads garlic, halved
olive oil
sea salt

Preheat the oven to 240°C (475°F). To roast the garlic, place in a small baking dish, drizzle with oil and sprinkle with salt. Cover and bake for 20 minutes or until soft.
While the garlic is roasting, place the oil in a non-stick frying pan over high heat. Add the onion and cook for 3–4 minutes or until golden. Remove from the pan and set aside.
Place the tomato slices in the pan and cook for 2 minutes on each side or until browned. Remove from the pan and set aside.
Place the steaks in the hot pan and cook for 1 minute on each side or to your liking. Remove from the pan and return the onion and tomato to the pan to reheat.
To serve, place a slice of toasted bread on each plate. Top with the steak and spread over some roasted garlic. Top with the onion and tomato and remaining slices of toast spread with roast garlic. Serves 4.

chicken poached in ginger broth

roast beef with sweet pumpkin

pizza with tomato, olives and rosemary

steak sandwiches with roasted garlic

blood plum tarts

parmesan shortbreads

sugar-roasted fruit

blood plum tarts

125g (4 oz) butter, softened
1/2 cup caster (superfine) sugar
2 eggs
1 teaspoon vanilla extract
3/4 cup ground almonds
1/3 cup plain (all-purpose) flour
4 blood plums, stones removed

Preheat the oven to 200°C (400°F). Process the butter and sugar in a food processor until smooth. Add the eggs, vanilla, almonds and flour and process until just combined. Place a plum in each of 4 individual ovenproof bowls. Spoon the almond mixture around the plum and bake for 15–20 minutes or until the filling is puffed and golden. Serves 4.

parmesan shortbreads

125g (4 oz) butter
1 cup plain (all-purpose) flour
1/3 cup grated parmesan cheese
1 teaspoon cracked black pepper

Preheat the oven to 170°C (325°F). Process the butter, flour, parmesan and pepper in a food processor until a smooth dough forms.
Place tablespoons of the dough on baking trays lined with non-stick baking paper. Bake for 15–20 minutes or until the shortbreads are lightly browned on the base.
Cool on wire racks. Serve with cheese and quince paste* after dinner. Makes 16 shortbreads.

sugar-roasted fruit

2 nectarines or peaches, halved
4 plums, halved
2 tablespoons sugar

Preheat the oven to 220°C (425°F). Place the nectarines or peaches and the plums in a baking dish lined with non-stick baking paper. Sprinkle with the sugar and bake for 20 minutes or until the sugar is golden.
Serve the roasted fruit with thick cream or vanilla-bean ice cream. Serves 4.

grilled ricotta and muscatel panettone sandwiches

1/3 cup marsala
1/3 cup seedless muscatels or raisins
8 slices panettone*
100g (3 1/2 oz) fresh ricotta cheese
icing (confectioner's) sugar

Place the marsala in a saucepan over medium heat and cook until simmering. Add the muscatels, remove the pan from the heat and allow to stand until the marsala has been absorbed.
Top half of the panettone slices with the muscatels, ricotta and another slice of panettone. Sprinkle with icing sugar and place on a preheated grill (broiler) or in a grill pan and toast for 1 minute each side or until golden. Serve with a good dessert wine or liqueur. Serves 4.
note – serve with the vanilla coffee on page 118 of the short top + sides chapter.

grilled ricotta and muscatel panettone sandwiches

coconut rice with lime syrup

1 cup long-grain rice
2½ cups (20 fl oz) water
¾ cup unsweetened coconut cream
2 tablespoons caster (superfine) sugar
lime syrup
¼ cup grated dark palm sugar*
½ cup (4 fl oz) water
¼ cup (2 fl oz) lime juice
1 tablespoon shredded lime rind
chilled unsweetened coconut cream to serve

Place the rice in a colander and wash well. Place the rice and water in a saucepan over medium-high heat and bring to the boil. Allow to simmer rapidly for 10 minutes or until almost all of the water has been absorbed. Add the coconut cream and caster sugar, cover, and cook over very low heat for 5 minutes.
While the rice is cooking, make the lime syrup. Place the palm sugar, water, lime juice and rind in a small saucepan over medium-low heat and allow to simmer for 4 minutes or until syrupy.
To serve, place the coconut rice in bowls and spoon over the syrup. Serve with chilled coconut cream. Serves 4–6.

cinnamon-crusted pancakes

1 quantity pancake batter (see page 164 of basics chapter)
½ cup sugar
1 tablespoon ground cinnamon
60g (2 oz) butter, melted

Place 3–4 tablespoons of the pancake batter in a non-stick frying pan over medium heat and cook until puffed and golden on both sides. Set aside and continue cooking the remaining mixture.
Combine the sugar and cinnamon in a shallow bowl. Brush both sides of the pancake lightly with the melted butter then press lightly into the sugar and cinnamon mixture on both sides.
Cook the sugar and cinnamon coated pancake in a non-stick frying pan over high heat for 45 seconds each side or until the sugar has melted and caramelised. Place on a plate and keep warm.
To serve, place a small stack of pancakes on each plate with a bowl of ice cream on the side. Serves 4–6.

coconut chocolate tarts

2 egg whites
½ cup sugar
2 cups desiccated coconut
filling
1¼ cups (10 fl oz) cream (single or pouring)
300g (10 oz) quality dark chocolate, chopped

Preheat the oven to 180°C (350°F). Place the egg whites, sugar and coconut in a bowl and mix to combine. Spray eight ¾ cup (6 fl oz) capacity deep muffin tins with non-stick cooking spray. With wetted hands or a spoon, press the coconut mixture into the tins, covering the base and sides to make a shell. Bake for 8–10 minutes or until the shells are just beginning to turn a light golden colour. Cool the shells for 1 minute then gently remove from the tins and place on a wire rack.
While the bases are cooking, make the filling. Place the cream in a saucepan over medium heat and cook until almost boiling. Remove from the heat and add the chopped chocolate, stirring until the chocolate has melted and the filling is smooth.
Pour the chocolate filling into the coconut tart shells and place in the freezer for 10 minutes or until the filling is set. Serve with coffee as a snack or with berries as a dessert. Makes 8 tarts.

little passionfruit cheesecakes

4 shortbread biscuits
topping
250g (8 oz) fresh ricotta cheese
250g (8 oz) cream cheese, chopped
2 eggs
½ cup sugar
2 tablespoons lime juice
⅔ cup fresh passionfruit pulp

Preheat the oven to 160°C (315°F). Place one shortbread biscuit in the base of 4 ramekins*. Process the ricotta, cream cheese, eggs, sugar and lime juice in a food processor until the mixture is smooth. Stir through the passionfruit pulp and spoon the mixture into the ramekins. Bake for 15 minutes or until the topping is firm. Serve warm or cold. Serves 4.

coconut rice with lime syrup

coconut chocolate tarts

cinnamon-crusted pancakes

little passionfruit cheesecakes

hort
top +
sides

morning

breakfast sandwich

milky porridge with berries

grilled sugar cinnamon doughnuts

morning

baked eggs

are simple and delicious. Line a few small bowls with blanched* baby English spinach leaves and sprinkle with sea salt and cracked black pepper. Break an egg into the centre of the spinach and bake in a preheated 180°C (350°F) oven for 12–16 minutes, depending on how you like the yolk cooked. Serve with hot buttered toast. You can also place mushrooms cooked in butter or slices of aged cheddar cheese in the bowl with the spinach.

soaked bircher

muesli is simple if you are an organised person. Make a batch of bircher muesli by placing 2 cups of quality muesli packed with grains, fruit and nuts in a bowl. Pour over 1 cup (8 fl oz) cream (single or pouring) and 1 cup (8 fl oz) milk and refrigerate overnight. Serve with sliced fresh fruit and extra milk.

toasted pistachio

and honey yoghurt is a perfect combination. Try thick, sweet honey poured into the base of small cups or bowls, sprinkled with roughly chopped toasted fresh pistachio nuts and then topped with lots of thick creamy yoghurt. Run your spoon down the side of the glass or bowl to the bottom and then drag it through the honey, nuts and yoghurt to get all three flavours.

vanilla coffee

is a great drink for the start or end of a perfect day. Place a drop or two of good-quality pure vanilla extract in your morning coffee before adding milk. For a real kick, add a generous teaspoon of vanilla to a strong short black after dinner. Thick and aromatic pure vanilla extract has the best flavour.

rhubarb and ricotta

on toasted warm raisin and cinnamon bread is a breakfast treat. Spread the toast with thick and creamy fresh ricotta. Top this with short lengths of rhubarb that have been simmered in orange juice until soft. Drizzle the whole lot lightly with honey or pure maple syrup. Eat fairly quickly so that the crisp toast doesn't go soggy.

breakfast sandwich

of crispy bacon, grilled sliced tomato, baby English spinach leaves and aged cheddar cheese. Place it all between toasted bread with substance, such as sourdough or grain bread. Wrap in napkins and serve in the lounge room or on the balcony soaking up the morning sun with newspapers, fresh juice and good coffee.

milky porridge

with berries to turn winter on its head. Top piping hot milky oat porridge with frozen blueberries and raspberries—easily found in the supermarket freezer—and then sprinkle with brown sugar and pour a milk float around the sides of the bowl. The berries will thaw in the hot porridge in no time, making the porridge the right temperature to tuck right into.

grilled sugar

cinnamon doughnuts are a very urban breakfast. Place readymade sugar and cinnamon coated doughnuts in a grill (broiler) pan and top with a plate to weight them down. Cook for 2 minutes each side or until the sugar has caramelised and the doughnut is toasted and crisp. Have this with a good strong coffee to start a busy day.

melon and coconut

frappés are the perfect way to stay cool on a hot summer morning. Blend chopped honeydew melon or rockmelon with a few sprigs of mint, a spoonful of unsweetened coconut cream and lots of ice until smooth, then pour into tall glasses for a summer morning pick up and chill out.

melon and coconut frappés　　　baked eggs

soaked bircher muesli

toasted pistachio and honey yoghurt

vanilla coffee

rhubarb and ricotta toast

lunchbox

little frittatas

Thai herb and chicken baguette

lunchbox pies

lunchbox

little frittatas

served hot or cold are great for a picnic or other portable occasion. A good base mixture is 6 eggs, 1 1/2 cups (12 fl oz) cream (single or pouring) and cracked black pepper. To this, add good things such as crispy bacon, parsley, grated quality cheddar cheese, pesto, roast pumpkin or potato pieces. Pour the mixture into deep non-stick muffin tins and bake at 180°C (350°F) for 20–30 minutes or until the frittatas are firm.

Thai herb

and chicken baguette is a new take on the chicken and mayo sandwich. Pack zingy Thai herbs such as Thai basil* , mint and coriander (cilantro) in sourdough baguettes with sliced grilled chicken and whole-egg mayonnaise mixed with lemon juice and cracked black pepper.

lunchbox pies

are great when you're on the move. Cut rounds of puff pastry and top with cooked chicken and roasted orange sweet potato (kumara) or sliced roast lamb and chutney. Cut larger rounds of pastry to cover. Seal the edges, place the pies on a baking tray and bake at 200°C (400°F) for 20 minutes or until puffed and golden. Serve warm or cold in lunchboxes with a fizzy drink or a rich-flavoured milk to quench a thirst.

chilli bean

tortilla sandwiches make a crisp snack with punch. Combine your favourite beans with chilli sauce and spread over a tortilla. Sprinkle with grated cheese and top with another tortilla. Place in a greased frying pan with a plate and a weight (such as a large can) on top and cook until crisp. Flip the tortilla and repeat until both sides are crisp and the filling is heated through.

simple tomato

sandwiches will always satisfy. Think fresh bread, ripe, red tomato slices, your favourite cheese, torn basil leaves, sea salt and cracked black pepper. We like this sandwich because there are only two decisions to make—which bread and which cheese.

grilled lime

and chilli chicken teamed with chilled Champagne. Cook the chicken pieces that have been marinating in chilli and lime juice under a hot grill (broiler) until tender and well browned. Place in boxes with lots of napkins and well-chilled tiny bottles of French Champagne. You'll be the envy of the picnic!

chocolate

cupcakes might not cover your five essential food groups, but you'll have the most popular lunchbox on the block. Fill the gaps with lollies and little chocolates and prepare to win friends and influence sweet tooths. Use the little chocolate brownies recipe on page 78 of the 20 minute chapter and cook them in patty cases.

risotto cakes

are easily made from leftovers of your favourite flavoured risotto. Make the cooled risotto into a flat patty in your hand. Place a piece of bocconcini or marinated fetta cheese in the middle and squash the risotto over the cheese to enclose. Shallow-fry the risotto cakes in hot oil until golden and crisp then drain on paper towel. Serve with a simple leaf salad or make small risotto cakes to go with drinks.

sticky banana

rice packed and rolled in paper makes this treat ready to go anywhere. Cook long-grain rice using the absorption method. Add 1/3 cup unsweetened coconut cream and sugar to taste, cover and allow the hot rice to stand for 4 minutes. Spread the rice along non-stick baking paper or banana leaves to form a flat rectangle. Place some finely chopped banana or mango down the centre and top with more rice to enclose the fruit. Roll up the paper or banana leaf.

chilli bean tortilla sandwiches

simple tomato sandwich

grilled lime and chilli chicken

risotto cakes

chocolate cupcakes

sticky banana rice

123

quick bite

garlic bruschetta

chilli popcorn

the wedge of cheese

quick bite

garlic bruschetta

made with a good wood-fired loaf of bread is a great example of simple is best. Drizzle with olive oil, grill until golden and crisp, then rub with a clove of garlic or a handful of basil. Top with thin slices of ripe tomato and slices of olive, goat's curd or a salad of shredded rocket (arugula), red onion and rinsed salted capers. Serve any time.

chilli popcorn

is great for video days on the sofa or to accompany a cold beer. Pop some popping corn in a hot frying pan, cover with a lid and toss with butter, sea salt and chilli powder while the popcorn is still hot. Great when there are lots of peckish people about, as you can make a huge bowl in just minutes.

the wedge

of cheese cannot be outdone. Serve just one cheese and avoid flavour clashes. If it's a great cheese, it can stand alone to make a simple supper. Whether it is a big gutsy blue or a ripe and runny Brie, purchase the best quality cheese you can find. Serve simple accompaniments such as oatcakes, wafers, dried Persian figs or sun-dried pears. Serve a suitably matched wine —blue cheese is great with a sticky botrytis-affected riesling, and Brie with a peppery young pinot noir.

jaffles

make the best quick snack. Toasted sandwiches never tasted so good. Use cheeses such as gruyère and cheddar, leftover roast chicken or roast lamb with onion marmalade, a whole egg (for the machines without the cut-in-half action) with double smoked ham and mustard, and the Sunday afternoon special—smoked ham, cheddar cheese and pineapple.

steamed pork

buns are a snap when purchased from the freezer section in Asian supermarkets. Steam them straight from the freezer for 10–15 minutes over rapidly boiling water and serve with hot chilli sauce. Often labelled as cha sui buns, or barbecue pork buns. Try different brands to find a good one.

goat's curd

flavoured with a little good fruity olive oil and a squeeze of lemon could be that special something you're looking for to go with that Sunday afternoon glass of red. Serve with warm bread or crackers.

spiced ricotta

and grilled figs can be made by mixing ground cinnamon and freshly grated nutmeg through fresh creamy ricotta. Sweeten the ricotta with a little sugar and spread over thickly sliced and toasted fruit bread. Top all this with sliced figs and sprinkle with brown sugar. Place under a hot grill (broiler) and cook until the sugar is caramelised and the figs are warm.

hot smoked

salmon salad is a great mixture of tastes and textures. Pile crunchy mixed lettuce leaves and sprigs of chervil high on plates. Break the salmon into large chunks, straight from the fillet. Top with a simple lemon and oil vinaigrette and serve with slices of sourdough bread.

coconut

macaroons are a simple one-bowl no-fuss cookie. Use the coconut base recipe for the coconut chocolate tarts on page 112. With wetted hands, press large tablespoons of the mixture into balls and place on a baking tray lined with non-stick baking paper. Flatten the coconut balls slightly and place in a preheated 180°C (350°F) oven and bake for 10–15 minutes or until the base is golden. Serve with coffee or hot chocolate.

jaffles

steamed pork buns

goat's curd

spiced ricotta and grilled figs

hot smoked salmon salad

coconut macaroons

127

evening

macaroni cheese

kitchen sink omelette

graze platter

evening

macaroni cheese

is perfect comfort food. Cook a couple of handfuls of macaroni in boiling water until tender, drain and return to the saucepan with a little cream or milk, mustard and cracked black pepper. Stir for 2 minutes over low heat then stir through some chopped flat-leaf parsley and place in ovenproof dishes. Top with grated cheese and lots of cracked black pepper. Bake until the cheese is melted and golden brown.

kitchen sink

omelette is my Dad's special for Sunday night. Take almost anything from the fridge that looks like a leftover—roast potatoes, pumpkin, roast lamb, cheese, tomatoes, whatever. Place them in a frying pan over medium heat and cook until warm. Beat some eggs and season with salt and pepper. Pour over the vegetables and stir to let the egg get to the bottom of the pan. Cook over low heat until almost set then grill (broil) the top. Cut into chunks and serve with hot buttered toast.

graze platter

of tasty morsels makes for a perfect relaxed dinner. A wedge of baked ricotta, paper-thin pancetta* or prosciutto*, tomato salad with basil and red onion, hommus or baba ghanoush, marinated olives and slices of good-quality bread. Team all this with a glass of good red to complete the story.

duck pancakes

are easy when you cheat a little and purchase a Chinese barbecue duck* from a good Chinese barbecue shop and ask them to chop it for you. While you are at the barbecue shop or near an Asian grocer, pick up some Peking pancakes from the freezer section or purchase them warm from a Chinese barbecue shop. Serve the duck warm with the warm pancakes, chopped green onions (scallions) and hoisin sauce.

ravioli

on baby spinach makes for dinner in a snap. Place baby English spinach or rocket (arugula) leaves in the bottom of pasta bowls. Cook good-quality fresh ravioli in plenty of boiling water until tender. Drain and place on the spinach or rocket leaves and top with a piece of butter, cracked black pepper and parmesan.

crisp potato

cakes with salmon are a simple and delicious meal. Grate 2 large potatoes into a bowl and mix with 2 tablespoons melted butter and 1 tablespoon chopped dill or parsley. Cook flattened spoonfuls of this mixture in an oiled pan until crisp and golden. Pile onto plates and top with smoked salmon or trout, watercress or similar greens and crème fraîche*.

chilli, garlic

and lemon spaghetti will fill a hungry stomach and is only minutes away. Just cook some pasta in a large saucepan of boiling salted water. Place a couple of tablespoons of fruity olive oil, some chopped chilli, sliced garlic and grated lemon rind in a frying pan and cook until fragrant. Toss with the cooked pasta. Anchovies, pepper and parmesan are optional extras.

steak sandwich

with brown onion rings and a spicy mustard is one of those things I sometimes crave. Toast thick slices of bread until golden. Place a few pieces of eye or scotch fillet into a very hot frying pan with a few onion rings and cook until the steak is cooked to your liking and the onion is golden and crisp. Place on the toasted bread with grain mustard and salad greens. Serve with crunchy potato chips if you are really hungry.

cheat's sushi

is easy—make the sushi rice using 1 cup short-grain rice and 2½ cups (20 fl oz) water. Cook over high heat until tunnels form in the rice then remove from the heat and cover tightly for 5 minutes. Place in a glass or ceramic bowl and stir through 3 tablespoons rice vinegar and a little sea salt. Cut nori sheets* into squares and top with some of the rice and your favourite sashimi slices. Serve with soy sauce and ginger.

duck pancakes

ravioli on baby spinach

crisp potato cakes with salmon

chilli, garlic and lemon spaghetti

steak sandwich

cheat's sushi

sides

asparagus with balsamic butter   roast garlic mash

warm walnut dressing over rocket

sides

asparagus

with balsamic butter makes the perfect side to many dishes. Simply melt a generous amount of butter in a frying pan over medium heat. Add some balsamic vinegar and a couple of bunches of trimmed asparagus. Cook until the asparagus is tender and serve with parmesan cheese and cracked black pepper.

roast garlic

mash potatoes with cream and butter are a comforting warm side for just about anything. Place a halved head of garlic in the oven. Sprinkle with olive oil and roast for about 30 minutes or until golden and soft. Squeeze the soft garlic from the skins. Boil peeled and chopped potatoes until soft. Mash with butter, sea salt, cream and most of the roast garlic. Top with more sea salt, melted butter and the last of the roast garlic. For a smooth creamy mash, press the potatoes through a 'mouli' food mill.

warm walnut dressing

over rocket (arugula) leaves will go with a simple pasta, grilled (broiled) meat, grilled anything. Place a good splash or two of olive oil in a small saucepan and add a big handful of walnuts and a few sprigs of rosemary. Place over low heat to infuse the flavours through the oil. Pour over the rocket leaves and finish with a squeeze of lemon juice, some cracked black pepper and a few olives. Serve immediately.

roast tomato

salad piled with torn basil leaves could even be served as a meal with some bread. Halve the tomatoes and place, flesh-side up, in a baking dish. Sprinkle with a little olive oil and pepper and bake in a preheated 200°C (400°F) oven until soft. Serve warm or cold with a big bunch of roughly shredded young basil leaves, balsamic vinegar, olive oil, more pepper and shaved parmesan cheese over the top.

greens

with oyster sauce go well with Asian-style dishes. Cook up a few tablespoons of shredded ginger in some sesame oil. Add ¼ cup (2 fl oz) oyster sauce, ¼ cup (2 fl oz) Chinese cooking wine* or dry sherry, ¼ cup (2 fl oz) salt-reduced soy and allow to simmer. Add brown sugar to taste. Blanch some Asian greens such as bok choy*, choy sum or gai larn* in boiling water for 10–20 seconds. Drain and place on a serving plate. Top with the sauce and serve.

salt and rosemary

baked potatoes are the perfect side to almost anything. Toss generous amounts of sea salt, olive oil and rosemary sprigs with baby new potatoes. Bake in a hot oven, shaking the pan once during cooking, until crunchy and golden on the outside and soft on the inside.

pine nut

butter with beans is a perfect combination. Place 80g (2¾ oz) butter in a saucepan and add a couple of tablespoons of chopped pine nuts. Cook over low heat until the butter and pine nuts are golden then add 2–3 tablespoons lemon juice. Pour the browned butter over vegetables such as steamed green beans, wilted spinach, blanched broccoli. Top with cracked black pepper and serve.

iceberg

salad is simple and easy. Remove the outer leaves from a crisp iceberg lettuce and discard. Halve the lettuce crosswise so you have a section of halved lettuce cups. Make a simple dressing of even quantities of oil and vinegar mixed with mustard, fresh herbs, sea salt and cracked black pepper. Pour the dressing over lettuce and serve. Before you start, if your lettuce is not as crisp as it needs to be, soak it in a large bowl of iced water to refresh.

sesame sweet

potato (kumara) will become a favourite. Brush the peeled long sweet potato slices with combined vegetable and sesame oil. Sprinkle with sea salt and place in a 200°C (400°F) oven and bake until the sweet potato is golden. Serve as a hot vegetable side or cool and serve with salad greens and a simple dressing.

roast tomato salad

greens with oyster sauce

salt and rosemary baked potatoes

pine nut butter with beans

iceberg salad

sesame sweet potato

sweet fix

ice cream with chocolate sticks

panna cotta

really real hot chocolate

sweet fix

ice cream

with chocolate sticks is a great way to be a big kid. Pile up scoops of your favourite flavoured good-quality ice cream. Serve with chocolate-covered stick biscuits to be used as the spoon. The spoon often accidentally gets eaten so have a pile of them on hand.

panna cotta

is easy to make en masse for large gatherings of friends. Place 1 split vanilla bean*, ¾ cup icing (confectioner's) sugar, 2 cups (16 fl oz) cream (single or pouring) and 1 cup (8 fl oz) milk in a saucepan over medium heat and bring almost to the boil. Soak 1 tablespoon gelatine in 3 tablespoons cold water. Whisk the gelatine into the cream mixture and allow to just bubble for 4 minutes. Pour into ramekins* or Chinese tea cups and refrigerate for 4–6 hours or until set. Serve with mixed berries in summer or wedges of sugar-grilled ruby grapefruit in winter.

really real hot chocolate

is the best and is made by placing chopped dark chocolate in the bottom of a tall glass. Pour in heated milk to almost fill the glass. Stir to melt the chocolate into the milk. Serve with extra chocolate on the side to nibble on—oooohhhh.

rice pudding

made in small bowls or ramekins* is fast and easy. Place 1–2 tablespoons cooked rice in the bottom of each bowl. Top with a whisked mixture of 4 eggs, ½ cup sugar, 2½ cups (20 fl oz) milk and 1 teaspoon vanilla extract. Place the bowls in a baking dish and half-fill the dish with hot water. Sprinkle with cinnamon or freshly grated nutmeg and bake in a preheated 160°C (315°F) oven for 20–25 minutes or until the puddings are just set. Eat warm or cold.

a chocolate wedge

of melt-in-your-mouth, drop-dead-delicious, couverture chocolate is irresistible. Place it on a sturdy platter or board in the middle of the table. Serve with utensils for breaking the chocolate such as an ice pick or knife. Accompany with a glass of torquay, liqueur muscat or port.

ice-cream sandwiches

made from good-quality shortbread or chocolate-coated biscuits and your favourite choice of ice cream are a simple but divine dessert. Sandwich between biscuits and refreeze for 5–10 minutes or until firm.

raspberry yoghurt

ice cream is a creamy ice delight with zing. Place 1kg (2 lb) thick plain yoghurt, 300g (10 oz) frozen raspberries, ¼ cup (2 fl oz) lemon or lime juice and 1 cup sugar in the bowl of an ice-cream machine and churn until frozen raspberry yoghurt appears. Serve with crispy wafers. Store any leftovers in a covered metal container in the freezer.

caramel pears

with pancakes will hit the spot on a cold afternoon or evening. Make pancakes from the batter on page 164 of the basics chapter. Cook some pear slices in 60g (2 oz) butter and 3 tablespoons brown sugar until soft. Layer the pears between the pancakes in a stack. Add an extra 3 tablespoons brown sugar to the pan with 1 cup (8 fl oz) cream (single or pouring). Allow to slowly simmer to make a thick caramel sauce. Pour over the pancake stack and serve.

quince jelly

on scones either made by you if you are feeling energetic or purchased from your favourite cake or pastry shop make a perfect morning tea. Place the scones, covered with a tea towel, in a warm oven if you have to reheat them. Serve with quince jelly or homemade strawberry jam—often found at street cake sales or fêtes and sold by older ladies wearing aprons of envy. Serve with thick cream or sweetened whipped cream on the side.

rice pudding

a chocolate wedge

ice-cream sandwiches

raspberry yoghurt ice cream

caramel pears with pancakes

quince jelly on scones

basics

roast

tomato

prosciutto + sage sauce

chilli + eggplant

basil soup

tools + tips

pepper grinder

I prefer a wooden grinder with a good adjustable screw for light or coarse grinding. If you purchase a good-quality pepper grinder, you'll probably never need to replace it.

deep frying pan

Use a deep frying pan with a heavy base. A frying pan has a larger surface area than a saucepan, therefore the liquid evaporates quickly, making the sauce thicker and more flavoursome, faster. If you only have a saucepan, you may need to simmer the sauce for longer than the recipe states.

measuring jugs

These are as important for measuring liquids as cups are for solids. Glass ones are good as you can also use them to ladle large amounts of liquid such as hot stock into risotto. Purchase jugs with measurements that are easy to read.

ripe cooking tomatoes

Purchase ripe or overripe tomatoes for cooking as they are sweeter and have more flavour. It is best to remove the skins before making a sauce, either by blanching the tomatoes in boiling water or peeling them with a sharp vegetable peeler. You may find that in the cooler months when tomatoes are not at their best, it is better to use canned tomatoes.

tips for success

• Depending on the time of year and what tomatoes are available, your sauce may be a little sharp or acid. This can be easily solved with a pinch or two of sugar • The basic sauce will have a thinner texture and sweeter taste if fresh tomatoes are used, whereas the canned tomatoes will result in a thicker sauce • Use tomato sauce to poach chicken or fish, as a sauce for vegetables or in lasagne, on pizza bases, or as a simple meal over hot pasta topped with grated parmesan cheese and cracked black pepper • When cooking the onions and garlic, don't let them brown as it will taint the delicate flavour of the sauce • When cooking with wine, be aware that poor-tasting wine will show through in the end product. This doesn't mean the vintage reds need to be opened, rather purchase an inexpensive bottle of reasonable quality • After cooking the tomato sauce, don't store or refrigerate it in the saucepan as the acid in the tomatoes may react with the metal in the saucepan • Some people believe that cooked tomato seeds taste bitter and remove all seeds from the tomatoes before cooking. They don't bother me personally, although I only cook tomato sauces using fresh tomatoes when they are well in season and are sweet and juicy.

canned tomatoes

Experiment with the brands available. Italian canned tomatoes are generally good. Look for the ones that are full of whole tomatoes in a thick juice. Avoid cans of chopped tomatoes as they are often a little slushy.

wooden spoons

You can never have enough wooden spoons. Keep them separate for sweet and savoury cooking. If the wooden spoon becomes tainted, put it through the dishwasher or soak for a few hours in a solution of vinegar and water. I like to keep a variety of sizes, too.

canned tomatoes

wooden spoons

deep frying pan

measuring jug   ripe cooking tomatoes

pepper grinder

classic tomato sauce

1
2
3
4

12 tomatoes or 4 x 440g (1 lb) cans peeled tomatoes, lightly crushed
1 tablespoon oil
1 clove garlic, crushed
2 small onions, chopped
1 cup (8 fl oz) red wine
2 tablespoons chopped oregano, basil or marjoram leaves
sea salt and cracked black pepper

STEP 1 If using fresh tomatoes, place in a saucepan of boiling water and cook for 1 minute. Drain, peel the skins and chop the flesh, reserving any liquid. If using canned tomatoes, there is no need to follow this step.

STEP 2 Heat the oil in a deep frying pan over medium–high heat. Add the garlic and onion and cook for 4 minutes or until soft.

STEP 3 Add the tomato, wine, herbs, salt and pepper and bring to the boil.

STEP 4 Allow the sauce to simmer for 20 minutes if using canned tomatoes and 35 minutes if using fresh tomatoes.

Refrigerate the sauce for up to 3 days. If you are not using the sauce within this time, freeze it in portion sizes ready to thaw and use. Tomato sauce can be frozen for 4–5 months.

ROAST TOMATO SAUCE Use only fresh tomatoes for this recipe. Halve them and place on an oiled baking tray cut-side up. Bake in a preheated 180°C (350°F) oven for 30 minutes or until soft. Follow the classic sauce recipe, adding the roast tomatoes instead of fresh or canned.

PROSCIUTTO AND SAGE TOMATO SAUCE Follow the basic recipe for the classic tomato sauce. After cooking the onion, add 6 slices roughly chopped prosciutto* and 2 tablespoons chopped sage leaves. Serve with extra grilled crisp prosciutto pieces.

TOMATO BASIL SOUP Follow the classic tomato sauce recipe and add 2 cups (16 fl oz) vegetable stock when adding the tomato. When this has simmered, stir through 1/3 cup basil (instead of the 2 tablespoons) and serve in deep bowls topped with pepper and parmesan cheese.

CHILLI AND EGGPLANT TOMATO SAUCE Add 2–3 sliced and seeded red chillies to the pan when cooking the garlic and onion. Chop 1 medium-size, young eggplant (aubergine) into large pieces and add with the tomato, following the classic tomato sauce recipe.

beef

chicken

stock

vegetable veal

fish

tools + tips

strainer

Use a fine strainer to remove cooking particles and small ingredients such as peppercorns from the stock. It is more practical to have a strainer that hooks or rests firmly on a pot or large bowl for easy straining.

skimming spoon or ladle

Use a large metal spoon to skim the surface of the stock and remove the cooking impurities that cloud its colour. You need to skim the stock, especially meat stocks, every 10–15 minutes when you first begin simmering it. Skimming frequently removes the fat and impurities that rise to the surface and stops them from bubbling back into the stock.

stockpot

A big stockpot or saucepan is essential for making stock. Stockpots vary in price, according to quality and size. If you only want to use the pot for stock, then a cheaper one will suffice. If you want to make other things in it, such as a big pot of shanks, you may find that the base of the pot is not very thick and that the contents will catch on the bottom of the pan. If so, purchase a multi-purpose stockpot with a substantially heavy base.

seasonings

Herbs such as rosemary, thyme, oregano and marjoram are also good for stocks. Use any combination of vegetables and herbs to create a stock. You may wish to tie herbs and peppercorns in muslin bags—often called a bouquet garni—for easy removal from the stock, although you can also strain the stock through a sieve.

vegetables

Use vegetables that are of good quality for a quality stock. Old vegetables will not give the same flavour as fresh ones. If you wish to use vegetables not in their prime, you will need to use more of them to create a well-flavoured stock. Vegetables such as leeks, mushrooms, parsnips, swedes and tomatoes are great to use in stocks.

muslin

Line a strainer or colander with fine muslin or cheesecloth to filter and clarify the stock. If you don't have muslin, use a fine strainer. Muslin is available from good cook shops and from fabric shops.

tips for success

• Do not allow the stock to boil—it should just simmer. If it boils, the result will be a fatty and cloudy stock
• Because cooking stock takes time, it is best to make large quantities and to freeze most of it in small portions. Make sure you label and date the stock. Frozen stock can be kept for up to 1 year if the content is fat free
• It is sometimes useful to allow the stock to simmer for another 2–3 hours or until it has doubled in strength. You can then use it as a more concentrated flavour or the stock can be frozen in a smaller quantity and water can be added later to return it to its original intensity • To remove fat from the top of warm stock, run a piece of paper towel over its surface. This soaks up most of the floating surface fat. Chill the stock to allow the fat to solidify on the top—the fat will then lift off easily
• When browning meat and vegetables for stock, be sure they are all well browned but not burnt. Adding burnt meat bones or vegetables to a stock will taint the flavour • Add salt towards the end of simmering stock. Adding salt at the beginning of cooking could result in an over-salty flavour once the water has been reduced from the stock.

strainer

vegetables

muslin

seasonings

stockpot

skimming spoon

chicken stock

3kg (6 lb) chicken bones
10 litres (320 fl oz) water
1½ cups (12 fl oz) dry white wine
1 onion, chopped
1 carrot, chopped
1 stick celery, chopped
8 black peppercorns
4 stalks parsley
2 bay leaves

STEP 1 Place the chicken bones and water in a large stockpot or saucepan over medium heat. Bring to a rapid simmer.

STEP 2 Add the wine, onion, carrot, celery, peppercorns, parsley and bay leaves and allow to slowly but constantly simmer.

STEP 3 Skim the surface of the stock with a spoon occasionally while it is cooking so that the stock remains clear.

STEP 4 Simmer the stock for 3 hours or until it is well flavoured. Strain the stock through a fine or muslin-lined sieve. Allow to cool and remove any solidified fat from the surface. Makes 5–6 litres.

To keep freshly made stock, cover and refrigerate for 2–3 days. After this time, the stock will need to be reboiled and it will then keep for up to 2 more days after this. Stock can also be frozen in small portions that are easy to thaw and use.

VEGETABLE STOCK Omit the chicken bones. Add to the basic recipe 2 chopped leeks and 1 cup sliced mushrooms. Follow the chicken stock recipe to finish. For a richer or darker vegetable stock, brown the lightly oiled vegetables in a preheated 200°C (400°F) oven for 30 minutes first.

VEAL STOCK Place 3kg (6 lb) chopped veal bones in a baking dish and brush with oil. Bake the bones in a preheated 200°C (400°F) oven for 30 minutes, then add the vegetables and bake for a further 30 minutes. Follow the chicken stock recipe, replacing the white wine with red wine.

BEEF STOCK Place 3kg (6 lb) chopped beef bones in a baking dish and brush with oil. Bake the bones in a preheated 200°C (400°F) oven for 30 minutes, then add the vegetables and bake for a further 30 minutes. Follow the chicken stock recipe, replacing the white wine with red wine.

FISH STOCK Use the heads and bones of three small non-oily fish such as snapper (instead of the chicken bones). Follow the chicken stock recipe, adding all the other ingredients. Simmer for 20 minutes only or the stock will be sour, then strain through muslin or a very fine strainer.

tempura

batter

pancakes crepes

beer

tools + tips

bowl

Use a dry bowl with high sides so that the batter stays in the bowl when you whisk it. You can place the bowl on a damp tea towel or kitchen cloth to stop it moving around on the bench while you are whisking.

drainer

Metal drainers are ideal for fishing food out of hot oil and for draining it before placing on paper towel. Choose traditional slotted spoon types, or try the bamboo and gold wire ones available in a variety of shapes and sizes in Asian supermarkets and good cook shops.

whisk

A wire balloon whisk is best. These come in varying sizes and it's good to have a small and large one. Whisks are great for everything from smoothing out sauces to beating egg whites the slow way. Whisking is a quick and easy way to remove lumps and incorporate air.

sifter

Use a sifter to remove any lumps from the flour. This will help to create a smooth batter when whisking in the liquid. Sifters come with a winding handle or a squeeze handle for ease of sifting. If you don't have a sifter, you can use a sieve and a spoon.

crepe pan

Great for making crepes, these medium-sized pans have gently sloping sides and are the perfect size. You can use a non-stick crepe pan, which won't need greasing. If you don't have a crepe pan, use a small shallow frying pan.

metal spatula

A spatula or slide makes for easy turning of pancakes and crepes or, if you're game, try your hand at flipping the batter with just the frying pan. I prefer a spatula with a wooden handle, although it seems the wider spatulas are only available with metal handles.

tips for success

• There is no need to leave batter to rest before using it. If you do, it may thicken and need extra liquid to thin it to a usable consistency
• Make sure you dry the foods to be dipped in batter so that the batter sticks well. If using a wet food, such as fish, you can coat it lightly in flour first
• The oil temperature is very important when deep-frying. It should be 190°C (375°F) to ensure that the food seals and is crisp and not soggy with oil
• Keep the cooked food or pancake stacks warm by placing them in a warm oven. Cover pancakes and crepes with a clean tea towel so they don't dry out
• Drain battered and fried foods on paper towel before serving to remove any excess surface grease.

cooking thermometer

For a crisp deep-fried batter, the oil must reach the correct temperature (190°C or 375°F). You can use a cooking thermometer that clips onto the side of your saucepan so that you can regulate the temperature accurately. These thermometers are also useful for making sugar syrups, jams, toffee and caramel.

metal spatulas

bowl and whisks

drainers

sifter

cooking thermometer

crepe pan

batter

2 cups plain (all-purpose) flour
sea salt
1 egg
1¹/₂ cups (12 fl oz) milk

STEP 1 Sift the flour and salt into a bowl and make a well in the centre.

STEP 2 Place the egg in a small bowl and beat lightly.

STEP 3 Add the egg and milk to the well in the flour and whisk until the batter is smooth. Add extra milk as necessary to create the desired consistency.

STEP 4 Use the batter to coat foods such as fish and vegetables, and deep-fry in hot oil until brown and crisp.

On standing, batter will thicken slightly—add more water or milk to return the batter to its original consistency. Batter without raising agents will keep covered in the fridge for up to 2 days. Batter with raising agents should be used soon after making, otherwise the raising agents will deactivate and the pancakes will not be light and fluffy.

PANCAKE BATTER Add an extra egg, 75g (2¹/₂ oz) melted butter, 3 teaspoons baking powder and ¹/₃ cup sugar to the basic batter mixture. Add the remaining ingredients following the basic recipe. Cook over medium heat in a non-stick frying pan until bubbles surface, flip and cook until golden.

BEER BATTER Replace the milk with 1½ cups (12 fl oz) cold beer and mix the batter until smooth. Use to make the classic beer-battered fish and chips. Use a premium beer with a good malty hops taste to ensure a well-flavoured batter.

CREPE BATTER Add 75g (2½ oz) melted butter and an extra cup (8 fl oz) of milk to the plain batter, to obtain the consistency of cream. Swirl a little batter in a small, greased crepe pan or frying pan and cook over medium heat until each side is lightly golden. Serve with lemon and sugar.

TEMPURA BATTER Replace the plain flour with 2 cups fine white rice flour and replace the milk with 1½ cups (12 fl oz) iced water and mix to a thin consistency. Use this batter to coat vegetables, prawns, fish and chicken strips. Serve with a readymade dipping sauce.

shortcrust

pastry

sweet

parmesan nut

pepper + mustard

tools + tips

food processor

This is the fast option for making pastry but if you don't have one, use cool fingertips in a rubbing motion to rub the butter through the flour. Use only the pulse button on the food processor in short bursts so that you don't over-process the flour and butter.

baking weights

You will need either baking weights, uncooked rice or dried beans to blind bake the pastry. Baking weights are small rounds of porcelain or metal and are reusable. Simply cool them after use then store in a sealable container. You can also keep a container of dried beans or rice for this same purpose, to be reused many times. Baking weights keep the pastry from bubbling when baked, creating a thin, even crust.

tart tins

These are available in a huge variety of shapes and sizes. Tart tins with loose bottom trays are the easiest to handle. You can also buy large metal rings that sit straight onto any baking tray to make a tart tin. After using, wipe clean and store. Scrubbing with detergents often scratches the surface and can cause the tins to rust.

pastry brush

Great for brushing the tops of pies or tart shells or for glazing the tops of tarts, these are available in many different sizes with synthetic or natural

pastry cutters

If you're going to use pastry cutters to make small tarts, make sure they're sharp and use them with one downward motion to give the pastry a clean edge.

rolling pins

These come in many different shapes and sizes, with or without handles. Use one that feels comfortable to you and apply even pressure with both hands for smooth and even rolling.

flour dredge

Useful for sprinkling a small and even amount of flour onto the work surface before rolling out dough. If the dough is a little sticky, use the flour dredge to lightly sprinkle a little flour over it to prevent it from sticking to the rolling pin. It's not essential but I do like to use one. You can also use your flour sifter or a sieve.

tips for success

• When combining the flour and butter in a food processor, use the pulse button and only process until large crumbs appear, then start adding the iced water
• Make sure the butter is hard and cold. Chop it into small pieces before using
• It's not necessary to knead the dough for a long time. A quick knead to get the pastry into a smooth ball is enough
• Before rolling, cover the bench with a light sprinkle of flour to ensure the pastry doesn't stick to the surface
• Do not stretch the pastry to fit into the tin. Fold the pastry over the rolling pin to lift it from the bench and then unroll it over the tart tin. Ease the pastry into the tin and this will prevent some shrinkage
• It is important to rest the pastry in the fridge after making it to keep the butter content cold and also to prevent the pastry from shrinking when it is baked. Cover the pastry with plastic wrap so that it doesn't dry out in the fridge
• Blind baking ensures the pastry stays crisp when used with a filling that contains moisture, such as a custard or other wet filling. If you're not using the blind-baked pastry shells the same day you bake them, store in an airtight container to keep them crisp
• When a blind-baked tart shell will be used with a moist filling, such as a sweet custard, keep the pastry from becoming soggy by brushing the warm pastry shell with a little egg white to seal it from the moisture.

pastry cutters

tart tins

pastry brushes

flour dredge

rolling pins

baking weights

169

shortcrust pastry

2 cups plain (all-purpose) flour
125g (4 oz) cold butter, chopped
iced water

STEP 1 Process the flour and butter in a food processor until the mixture has formed rough crumbs. (Do not over-process or the dough will become too sticky.)

STEP 2 While the motor is running, add enough iced water to form a soft dough. Remove from the food processor and knead lightly. Wrap in plastic wrap and refrigerate for 30 minutes to prevent the pastry from shrinking when baked.

STEP 3 Roll out the pastry on a lightly floured surface or on a sheet of non-stick baking paper until 2–3mm (1/8 in) thick. Line the desired tin or tins with the pastry, easing it into the shell without stretching it. Chill the pastry in the tin for 5 minutes.

STEP 4 Blind bake the pastry: prick the base and the sides of the pastry with a fork, cover with a sheet of non-stick baking paper and fill the tin with baking weights or dried beans or rice. Bake the pastry case in a preheated 190°C (375°F) oven for 5 minutes. Remove the weights and paper, and return the pastry to the oven for a further 5 minutes or until a light golden colour.

If using the pastry within 3 days, store the cooked shell in an airtight container. To keep the pastry shell for longer, wrap in plastic wrap and freeze for up to 3 months. Thaw and re-crisp the pastry in a 180°C (350°F) oven for 3–5 minutes before using. You can also freeze the uncooked pastry shell in the tin for up to 3 months. To use, thaw the pastry and follow the blind-baking instructions in step 4 above.

SWEET SHORTCRUST PASTRY The simplest variation of the lot. Just add 3 tablespoons of caster (superfine) sugar to the flour before processing. This is your stock standard pastry for any sweet tart or pie and can be filled with anything from lemon curd to rich chocolate ganache.

NUT SHORTCRUST PASTRY Add ⅓ cup ground nuts such as almonds, hazelnuts or walnuts to the flour before processing. For a sweet version, add 2 tablespoons caster (superfine) sugar as well. Try savoury fillings with rich cheeses. The sweet version can be filled with just about anything.

PARMESAN SHORTCRUST PASTRY Add 1/3 cup grated parmesan cheese to the flour before processing. Use this pastry for savoury tarts or pies, such as a tart spread with fresh goat's curd or fresh ricotta and topped with roast tomatoes and sliced olives or pesto.

PEPPER AND MUSTARD SHORTCRUST PASTRY Add 1 teaspoon cracked black pepper and 2 tablespoons seeded mustard before processing the flour. Use this pastry for savoury fillings of vegetables and cheeses or for adding a kick to a standard recipe such as an egg and bacon pie.

olive

dough

muscatel + cinnamon

pizza

calzone

tools + tips

rolling pins

These come in a variety of shapes and sizes and materials such as wood, plastic, marble and steel. Make sure that you feel comfortable using it to roll an even dough. There is no need to wash wooden rolling pins, simply wipe clean and remove any sticky dough using a pastry scraper or blunt knife.

dough hook

If you have a set of beaters on a stand that came with your electric mixer, check if there is a dough hook attachment. If not, think about getting one when purchasing your next mixer, as this attachment takes most of the hard work out of making dough. A single dough hook is more effective than using an electric mixer with two beaters. You can use the dough hook to make the dough and then knead it manually, reducing time and muscle action.

seeds

Seeds can be kneaded into the dough before baking for flavour, or sprinkled over a dough that has been brushed with oil, water or egg. Seeds to try include sesame, linseed, poppy, sunflower and pumpkin.

flour

You can use many different flours to create a base dough. Flours such as soya, rye, wholemeal and chickpea can be used. With heavier flours such as rye, soya and chickpea, you can use half plain (all-purpose) flour and half of the heavier flour so that the dough is not too dense.

tips for success

• Always add lukewarm water to the yeast mixture. If the temperature is hotter, it may kill or deactivate the yeast • Yeast is a living organism that needs sugar, its form of food, to activate, but too much sugar will also kill the yeast, as will salt • When kneading, fold the front of the dough to the middle, press it into the centre and then press forward with your hand. Use the other hand to give the dough a quarter turn and repeat the process until the dough is smooth and elastic • The dough is kneaded sufficiently when it feels smooth and elastic. If you press it with your thumb, it should bounce back • When yeast is proving, keep it covered and warm, away from draughts, but don't let it get too hot or the yeast will die. The optimum temperature for yeast to grow is 27°C (80°F) • Cool cooked bread on wire racks for a crisp crust • The dough needs to be kneaded sufficiently so that the gluten strands in the flour are developed and elastic. Then when the yeast gives off its carbon dioxide, it will stretch and hold like a framework • Add sugar, fruits, vegetables and other flavourings after the first rising of the dough to avoid destroying the yeast.

muscles

Make sure yours are in good working order if you don't have an electric mixer with a dough hook or just for the normal kneading and rolling that making dough requires.

yeast

I prefer dry yeast for convenience, but make sure it hasn't run past its expiry date or it may not activate. The first step in the basic dough recipe is a good test to ensure the yeast is alive, as the bubbles on the surface of the mixture signal activity. Yeast needs warmth, sugar and moisture to grow. Too much heat, sugar, salt or fat may kill it. Yeast works by releasing tiny bubbles of carbon dioxide which cause the dough to stretch and rise.

rolling pin

seeds

dough hook

yeast

flours

tins

dough

1 teaspoon active dry yeast
pinch sugar
2/3 cup (5¹/2 fl oz) lukewarm water
2 cups plain (all-purpose) flour
1/2 teaspoon sea salt
1/4 cup (2 fl oz) olive oil

STEP 1 Place the yeast, sugar and water in a bowl and mix to combine.
Stand the mixture in a warm place until there are bubbles on the surface.

STEP 2 Place the flour, salt, oil and yeast mixture in the bowl. Use an electric mixer
fitted with a dough hook or a bowl and wooden spoon and mix well until a
smooth dough forms.

STEP 3 Knead the dough with the dough hook for 5 minutes or by hand on a
lightly floured surface for 25 minutes or until it is smooth and elastic.

STEP 4 Place the dough in a clean, oiled bowl, cover with a damp clean tea towel,
and allow to stand in a warm place for 20 minutes or until it has doubled
in size. Knead the dough lightly before shaping and placing in a tin.
Cover and allow to stand until it has doubled in size. Bake in a preheated
200°C (400°F) oven for 25 minutes or until golden and hollow sounding
when tapped.

If you are not using the dough after the proving* stage, wrap it tightly in plastic
wrap and place it in the freezer to arrest the growth of the yeast. Before shaping
and baking, allow the dough to thaw and knead it lightly. Always allow the dough to
prove a second time before baking. Dough to be baked in a loaf can be shaped
and frozen in the tin—simply thaw the dough and allow it to prove before baking.
If adding flavourings to the dough, add them after the dough has defrosted, before
the second proving. Dough can be kept frozen for up to 3 months.

CALZONE Divide the risen dough into 4 portions. Roll on a floured surface until 1cm (1/2 in) thick. Place fillings, such as cheeses, grilled vegetables or meats and pesto, on half of the dough. Fold over the dough to enclose the filling. Bake in a preheated 200°C (400°F) oven for 25 minutes or until golden.

PIZZA BASES Divide the risen dough into 4 equal portions and roll on a lightly floured surface until the desired thickness. Add toppings and bake in a 200°C (400°F) oven for 15–20 minutes or until the base is golden and the topping is cooked.

OLIVE BREAD Roll the risen dough on a floured surface until 2cm (¾ in) thick. Place on a baking tray. Press in a few olives and rosemary sprigs. Sprinkle with salt and olive oil. Cover with a damp tea towel; stand until doubled in size. Bake in a preheated 200°C (400°F) oven for 20 minutes.

MUSCATEL + CINNAMON BREAD Knead 1 cup seedless muscatels, 2 tablespoons sugar and 2 teaspoons ground cinnamon into the dough. Place in a small loaf tin. Cover with a damp tea towel and allow to stand until doubled in size. Bake in a preheated 200°C (400°F) oven for 35 minutes.

glossary

amaretto

Almond-flavoured liqueur with a slightly bitter taste. Substitute almond essence if unavailable.

angel hair pasta

A very thin, tubular pasta—hence its name. Substitutes include spaghetti, linguine and thin fettuccine. Available fresh or dry, plain or flavoured.

arborio rice

Taking its name from a village in the Piedmont region of northern Italy, this short-grain rice is used for risotto. It releases some of its starch when cooked, making a creamy savoury rice dish. Other varieties used for risotto include violone and carnaroli. All may be labelled simply as risotto rice.

Balmain or Moreton Bay bugs

Small flat Australian crustaceans with a peculiar body appearance. The sweet and delicate tail meat is similar to a small lobster or crayfish. All of the meat is found in the tail which is easily removed in one piece. They can be purchased green (raw) or cooked. Substitute with langoustines (shrimp), small lobster tails or large prawns (shrimp).

bamboo steamer

An Asian bamboo container with a lid and a slatted base. Placed on top of a saucepan of boiling water, the steamer holds the food to be steamed. A metal steamer can also be used. Available from Asian food stores and most cook shops.

blanching

A cooking method in which foods are plunged into boiling water for a few seconds, removed and then refreshed under cold water which stops the cooking process. Used to heighten the colour and flavour, to firm flesh and to loosen skins.

bocconcini

Fresh Italian mozzarella balls sold in a water or brine solution. Available from delicatessens and supermarkets. Traditionally made from buffalo milk but more commonly found made from cow's milk.

bok choy

A mildly flavoured green also known as Chinese chard or Chinese white cabbage. Limit the cooking time so that it stays green and slightly crisp.

caper berries

The flower of the caper bush becomes an oval berry or fruit which is full of tiny seeds. Caper berries are sold with their tender stems attached in vinegar or a brine solution. Available from good delicatessens.

cellophane noodles

Cellophane or beanthread noodles are made from the starch of mung beans and come as vermicelli or as flat, wide noodles. They are difficult to cut and separate when dried, so buy them in small bundles if possible. They need to be soaked in boiling water for 10 minutes or until soft, and then drained. You can also deep-fry them straight from the packet.

chervil

A delicate, lacey-looking herb with a faint, sweet aniseed flavour. Its flavour diminishes after being chopped, so add to food just before serving.

chilli oil

Oil infused with the heat and flavour of chillies. It often has a red tinge. Different brands have different strengths so check them for heat by tasting a drop before using. Available from Asian food stores and delicatessens.

Chinese barbecue duck

A cooked duck, spiced and barbecued in the traditional Chinese barbecue style. Available from Chinese barbecue shops and Chinese food stores.

Chinese barbecue pork

Cooked pork meat, spiced and barbecued in the traditional Chinese barbecue style. Available from Chinese barbecue shops and Chinese food stores.

Chinese cooking wine

A cooking wine made from rice which is similar to dry sherry. Often labelled as shao hsing in Asian supermarkets.

Chinese five spice powder

An equal mixture of the spices cinnamon, anise pepper, star anise clove and fennel. Available from most supermarkets and Asian food stores.

crème fraîche

A mixture of soured cream and fresh cream. Lighter and not as thick as the easily obtainable sour cream although this does make a good substitute.

demerara sugar

A dark sugar with hard, dry crystals. The colour comes from molasses. Substitute dark brown sugar if necessary.

fish sauce

Clear, amber-tinted liquid that is drained from salted, fermented fish. A very important flavouring in Thai cuisine. Available from supermarkets and Asian food stores.

fresh rice noodles

Fresh rice noodles come in a variety of widths and lengths and are located in the refrigerator section of Asian food stores and some supermarkets. Keep them only for a few days in the refrigerator. To prepare, soak noodles in hot to boiling water for 1 minute, separating them gently with a fork, then drain. Fresh rice noodles also come as rolls which can be steamed as a side dish or filled and steamed.

gai larn

Also known as Chinese broccoli or Chinese kale. A leafy vegetable with dark green leaves and small white flowers. The stout stems can be steamed, braised, boiled or stir-fried.

gravlax

From Nordic origins, a salmon fillet that has been cured in a combination of rock salt, sugar and herbs. It is then sliced thinly and resembles smoked salmon, but has a more delicate flavour. Available in good delicatessens and some supermarkets.

haloumi

Fine white cheese made from sheep's milk. It has a stringy texture and is usually sold in brine. Available from delicatessens and some supermarkets.

harissa

A hot paste of red chillies, garlic, spices and olive oil. Available in tubes or jars from delicatessens.

hoisin sauce

A thick, sweet-tasting Chinese sauce made from fermented soy beans, sugar, salt and red rice. Use as a dipping sauce or glaze. Traditionally used for Peking duck. Available from Asian food stores and supermarkets.

Hokkien noodles

Round yellow wheat noodles available from the refrigerator section of supermarkets and Asian food stores. Place in a bowl and cover with hot to boiling water. Soak for 1–2 minutes or until the noodles have softened, and then drain.

hommus

A paste made from chickpeas, tahini, olive oil, garlic and lemon juice, from the Middle Eastern countries. Used as a spread or dip.

jap pumpkin

A very sweet and soft variety of pumpkin with a distinctive green and white striped skin.

juniper berry

A dark-coloured mild spiced berry that complements game and red meats. Crush lightly before use to release the flavour. Available as a moist dried berry from good delicatessens and spice shops.

kaffir lime

The fragrant leaves are crushed or shredded and used in cooking and the limes are used for their juice, mainly in Thai cuisine. Available as packets of leaves or as limes from Asian food stores.

laksa paste

The base to a rich Asian coconut milk soup. A laksa paste can contain ground spices, herbs, ginger, shrimp paste and lemongrass. The soup contains a spiced coconut broth, noodles, vegetables such as beansprouts, mint and coriander (cilantro), seafood or chicken. Laksa paste is available from supermarkets and Asian food stores. You may need to try a few to find a good brand.

lemongrass

A tall, lemon-scented grass used in Asian, mainly Thai, cooking. Peel away the outer leaves and use the tender root end of the grass. Chop finely or use in pieces to infuse flavour and remove from the dish before serving. Available from Asian food stores and fruit and vegetable shops.

linguine

Long, thin pasta with square cut

edges. Similar to flat spaghetti. Substitute spaghetti or fettuccine.

mascarpone

An Italian, triple-cream, curd-style fresh cheese, which has a similar consistency to double or thick cream. Available from good delicatessens and some supermarkets.

miso

A thick paste made from fermented and processed soy beans. Red miso is a combination of barley and soy beans, and white or yellow miso is a combination of rice and soy beans.

muscato d'asti

A fruity sparkling Italian dessert wine generally with flavours of stone fruit and citrus. Low in alcohol content, this is also said to be the perfect breakfast wine.

nori sheets

Dried seaweed pressed into square sheets. Use for nori rolls, soups and Japanese cuisine. Keep dry and store in an airtight container. Available in packets from Asian food stores.

palm sugar

Sap of the palm tree concentrated into a heavy, moist sugar. Sold in block form and should be grated or shaved before using. Used mainly in Thai cooking. I prefer the darker one for its stronger caramel flavour. Substitute brown sugar.

pancetta

Italian rolled and cured meat similar to prosciutto only not as salty or as tough. Can be eaten in thin slices from the roll or cooked in dishes.

panettone

An aromatic northern Italian yeast bread made with raisins and candied peel, panettone is traditionally eaten at Christmas, when large and small versions are found in most Italian delicatessens or large supermarkets.

pasta

3 cups plain (all-purpose) flour
4 large eggs
2 teaspoons salt

Place the flour on a bench top in a mound. Make a hole in the mound and break the eggs into the hole. Add the salt, break the eggs up with a fork and work into the flour. (You can do this step in a food processor.) Place the dough on a lightly floured surface (you may need to add a little flour to make the dough manageable) and knead until smooth. Cut the pasta into 4 pieces and roll through a pasta machine or using a rolling pin until the desired thickness. Cut the pasta into shapes or cover with a damp cloth if you are using it a few hours later. Cook the pasta in plenty of boiling water until al dente. Make sure the water stays boiling while the pasta cooks. To dry, hang the pasta over a suspended wooden spoon or a clean broom handle for 1–2 hours, until dry and hard. Store the pasta in airtight containers. Makes 1 quantity.

preserved lemon

Originally from the Middle Eastern countries, these are whole lemons preserved in salt and lemon juice. Remove the flesh and white pith, using only the rinsed rind.

prosciutto

A type of Italian 'ham' which has been salted and air dried. Sold in paper thin slices for eating raw or for using in cooked dishes.

proving

Process when a yeast mixture or dough is left covered in a warm draught-free place to rise or prove.

quince paste

A thick and fragrant paste made from quinces, sugar and lemon juice. It is often sliced and served with cheese. Available from good delicatessens.

ramekins

Small, ovenproof dishes used for soufflés, crème brûlées, and other individually served foods.

red curry paste

A hot and spicy paste of ground red chillies, herbs and spices. Available in bottles from supermarkets or Asian food stores.

rice paper rounds

Fine transparent circles made from a paste of rice and water. Before using, brush or dip in warm water until they are pliable. Available from Asian food stores.

roma tomatoes

Also known as egg, Italian or plum tomatoes. These oval tomatoes have good flavour, making them great for cooking and eating.

sashimi tuna

Finest quality tuna cut in an Asian or Japanese style. It is very tender and is used raw in Japanese cuisine. Often used sparingly due to price. Available from good fish markets.

semi-dried tomatoes

Wedges of ripe tomato that have been semi-sundried so they are still soft and moist. Often sold in flavoured oil. Available from some supermarkets and delicatessens.

shiitake mushrooms

Originally from Japan and Korea, these mushrooms have a distinctive, full-bodied flavour. They have brownish tops with creamy undersides. Available from good fruit and vegetable stores.

star anise

A star-shaped spice with a sweet aniseed flavour. Often used in Asian and Indian cooking. Available also as a powder. Purchase from Asian food stores or spice shops.

Thai basil

Includes many varieties such as holy, purple and sweet. Any of these can be used in Thai or Asian cuisine. Substitute any type of basil.

tortillas

Cornbread baked in flat discs used to wrap foods or eaten as bread. Wheat flour tortillas are another popular variety. Traditionally from Mexico and South American countries. Available in varying sizes from supermarkets.

udon noodles

White Japanese wheat noodles, which can be purchased fresh (from the refrigerator section) or dried. They come in a variety of thicknesses and lengths. Available from Japanese or Asian food stores.

vanilla beans

Cured pods from the vanilla orchid. Used whole, often split, to infuse flavour into custard or cream-based recipes. Also available is pure vanilla extract, which is a thick, dark, sticky liquid, and makes a good substitute for vanilla beans (use 1 teaspoon vanilla extract per vanilla bean needed.

Vietnamese mint

Not a member of the mint family although it is called mint. It has long, green narrow leaves with purple markings. It is bitter, zesty and pungent in flavour. Available from Asian food stores.

wasabi

A spice that comes from the knobbly root of the Japanese plant *Wasabia japonica*. A traditional condiment served with Japanese sushi and sashimi. It has the same warming or nasal-stinging sensation as horseradish. Available as a paste or powder from Asian food stores.

conversion chart

1 cup = 250ml (8 fl oz)
1 Australian tablespoon = 20ml (4 teaspoons)
1 UK tablespoon = 15ml (3 teaspoons)
1 teaspoon = 5ml

CUP CONVERSIONS
1 cup baby English spinach = 60g (2 oz)
1 cup basil leaves, whole, firmly packed = 50g (1¾ oz)
1 cup cheese, parmesan, finely grated = 100g (3½ oz)
1 cup chickpeas = 220g (7 oz)
1 cup unsweetened coconut cream = 250g (8 oz)
1 cup coconut, dessicated = 90g (3 oz)
1 cup coriander (cilantro) leaves, whole = 30g (1 oz)
1 cup couscous = 200g (6½ oz)
1 cup flour, white = 125g (4 oz)
1 cup lentils = 200g (6½ oz)
1 cup olives, stoned = 155g (5 oz)
1 cup parsley, flat-leaf, whole = 20g (¾ oz)
1 cup polenta = 150g (5 oz)
1 cup rice, raw = 220g (7 oz)
1 cup rocket (arugula) leaves, roughly chopped = 45g (1½ oz)
1 cup sugar, caster (superfine) = 220g (7 oz)
1 cup sugar, white = 250g (8 oz)

index